KU-019-796

Quentin Letts is political sketch writer for *The Times* and theatre critic for the *Sunday Times*. A regular broadcaster on radio and television, he was formerly New York correspondent for *The Times*, gossip columnist for the *Daily Telegraph* and parliamentary sketch writer for the *Daily Mail*. He is the author of the *Sunday Times* bestseller *50 People Who Buggered Up Britain*. His hobbies are gossip, hymn-singing and cricket. He lives in rural Herefordshire.

STOP BLOODY BOSSING ME ABOUT

How We Need to Stop
Being Told What to Do

Quentin Letts

CONSTABLE

CONSTABLE

First published in Great Britain in 2021 by Constable
This paperback edition published in 2021 by Constable

1 3 5 7 9 10 8 6 4 2

Copyright © Quentin Letts, 2021

The moral right of the author has been asserted.

All rights reserved.

No part of this publication may be reproduced, stored in a retrieval system,
or transmitted, in any form, or by any means, without the prior permission in
writing of the publisher, nor be otherwise circulated in any form of binding or
cover other than that in which it is published and without a similar condition
including this condition being imposed on the subsequent purchaser.

A CIP catalogue record for this book
is available from the British Library.

ISBN: 978-0-34913-517-5

Typeset in Sabon by Hewer Text UK Ltd, Edinburgh
Printed and bound in Great Britain by Clays Ltd, Elcograf, S.p.A.

Papers used by Constable are from well-managed
forests and other responsible sources.

Constable
An imprint of
Little, Brown Book Group
Carmelite House
50 Victoria Embankment
London EC4Y 0DZ

An Hachette UK Company

www.hachette.co.uk

www.littlebrown.co.uk

For my daughter-in-law, Xiaolei – 欢迎来到英国

Contents

Foreword
by Flip

'Fenton! Fenton!! Fentooooooooooooon!!! Jesus Christ!'
   Many of you will have seen the YouTube footage of
Fenton the black Labrador scattering deer in Richmond
Park. Whose side were you on? Fenton's? Or that of the
exasperated man trailing after him, oathing like an
anchorite with a stubbed toe?

For those who have not seen the clip, here is what happens. It is a November 2011 morning in Richmond Park, south London. The camera belongs to a nature lover who is filming deer thirty yards away. In the distance we see the road that cuts through the park. It has its usual burden of traffic as people head to work. Otherwise the scene is bucolic. Nature reigns. Since AD 1637 this expanse of grassland has been grazed by red and fallow deer, bringing a touch of the wild to prosaic suburbs, Norbiton to the south, Twickenham and Wimbledon to west and east. The camera advances delicately on the deer, not wishing to disturb them. We hear the soft tread of boot on grass and the occasional crunch of fallen leaves. Until: 'Fenton! Fenton!! Fentooooooooooooon!!!' The camera pans unsteadily towards the source of these exasperated shouts. We can make out a streak of something black and canine. The deer take flight. More beasts come running from the right. Fenton has been busy. He has, lucky fellow, started a stampede. By now the man's cries, quite posh, are a mixture of anger, despair and horror as the deer gallop towards the road, hooves drumming. They leap across the tarmac and Fenton keeps chasing. The camera finally shows us the back of Fenton's owner trotting helplessly after the merry caboodle, hissing, 'Oh Chrissssssst.'

The video always makes me wag my tail. This is no doubt irresponsible. The 'correct' response would probably be to whimper and stick that tail between one's legs. But Fenton's disobedience is just too liberatingly wonderful. What made it even better was discovering that he was a sometime guide dog for the blind. Then the cherry on the

Bakewell tart: Fenton's owner, Max Findlay, was a lawyer who wrote for those two outlets of prissy propriety, the *Financial Times* and the *Observer*. When approached about the incident, he snapped that he certainly did not wish to discuss the matter.

Why is the Fenton clip funny? In part it is the spectacle of middle-class authority unravelling, all the sweeter from one of those London legal types who seem like they have everything arranged to their creamy satisfaction. Who knows what lawsuits flashed through that highly trained Findlay mind when Fenton took off after the deer? And Fenton is an example of capture off its leash. All those years of being the dutiful guide dog must have driven him to distraction. Guide dogs are assumed to be the saintliest of God's creations. Aw, look, a nice guide doggy, pat pat pat. Underneath the harness they are just as naughty as the rest of us. At last Fenton let his coat down. Instinct seized his heart and he ignored the man who fancied himself his master.

My daughter and I have lived with the Letts family in Herefordshire for several years. As a former trained killer I am happy to wish this book well – and certainly glad to see the bloody thing finished. Maybe we can now have more walks. The book is for those who find Fenton an inspiration. Those who take Mr Findlay's side may want to take it back to the bookshop and trade it in for something by Dame Polly Toynbee.

Kennel 1, The Old Mill,
How Caple, December 2020.

Introduction

We have been infantilised. Wash your hands, don't eat sweets, no outdoor games. Cover your faces, bend that knee. Comply. Conform. Surrender your humanity to masks. And as individualism and dynamism duly wither and the economy tanks, watch your pensions shrivel till they're the size of squirrels' nuts.

It has been a bossy couple of years. Supermarket tannoys told shoppers they were heroes, simply for standing six feet apart, and then said they couldn't buy tampons because those were 'non-essential items'. Child-art rainbows were daubed on delivery lorries, instructing us to think milky thoughts about the health service. If we didn't clap for nurses, neighbours squealed. A once freedom-loving prime minister said 'lose weight', even while the Treasury was subsidising pub grub. Sugar was taxed. It would only go and rot our molars and then we'd have to visit the dentist – who had been forced to shut by pandemic-hygiene edicts. One way or another we were toothless.

Authority frets about salt intakes, drinking habits (one fizzy drink a week quite enough for you, Jemima) and five-a-day-fruit-or-veg. The whole country's farting like the Household Cavalry. No wonder the air quality's gone awry. When my parents ran a school they kept a ledger on pupils' lavatory habits – 'have you done a number two today, Blenkinsop?' Nurse Hancock, secretary of state for bowels, would probably have started asking the same question had he not come such a glorious cropper. Oh, baby, wasn't that a wonderful pratfall?

Ministers, officials and scientists ceased caring about popular will and started imposing their own. The elected legislature turned turtle, and we had government by bossocracy: a caste of poohbahs who reckoned they knew best. They did it by whipping up fear. Kenneth Clark, in *Civilisation*, writes that fear is a killer. 'Civilisation is actually quite fragile. It can be destroyed. What are its enemies? Fear – fear of war, fear of invasion, fear of plague and famine, that make it simply not worthwhile constructing things, or planting trees, or even planning next year's crops. And fear of the supernatural, which means that you daren't question anything or change anything.'

'Fear of plague' indeed became government policy and it quickly ruined much that made life fun. We no longer sang or worshipped together. We no longer kissed or met friends. The supernatural may nowadays be little considered by officialdom, but it has been replaced by the plastic deity of correctitude, whose dismal activists impose their views with moral terrorism. When so much is subjected to disapproval, we stop offering. Why volunteer when you must prove you are not a child molester? Why start a business when so much woke crapola is thrown in your way? When British police push an old woman into the back of a paddy wagon for silently complaining about her infringed liberties, can't they see that they rather prove her point? What the hell is happening to our country?

This is not a libertarian book. I accept the basic contract between subject and Crown. I pay my taxes. Taken discretely, rules often make sense. But there comes a point when, on top of the clamour of employers' demands, civic interdictions and – ping! – constant advisories from our hectoring mobiles, the hassle of regulation becomes overwhelming: a screaming, scraping white noise of emergency prohibitions and snoopery. Privacy is dead. Free speech is in intensive care. The boozer was shut, abroad was closed and for much of 2020 you couldn't buy a pint of milk unless yashmaked like Dick Turpin. For an entire season we were not even allowed to go to county cricket, even though you were more likely to die of hypothermia than catch the virus from a few other egg-sandwich munchers at any wind-blown ground.

Covid put the turbochargers on an authoritarianism that had been creeping up on us for a while. Officialdom, having seized new powers, made clear it would not surrender them once the pandemic was on the wane. Rules are a narcotic, both for boss-cats and, alas, for many of those being told what to do. Timid as pink-eared mice in a psychology lab, citizens continued to obey Covid directives long after the social-distancing floor stickers had faded. Civil servants urged the rest of us to return to the office but they themselves kept working from home, invoking 'safety'. 'Idleness', more like.

A generation ago it was seatbelts in cars and 'smoking

can damage your health' panels on fag packets. Soon we were told to stop watching Benny Hill. Men had to attend birthing suites. Now the 'isms' are cults and the commonest word on the airwaves is 'must'. The people using it still call themselves liberals but flowery sixties liberalism, sweet and stoned, has been bastardised into an intolerance stiffer than the stuff-shirt order of old. You are racist if you chuckle at unconscious bias. You are anti-trans if you use the word 'woman'. During the early days of lockdown you were as bad as a killer if you kissed your octogenarian mum. Gauleiter activism bullies us with moral terrorism, politicians are too wet to resist and the bossocracy prospers.

Well, sod it. Enough is enough. I've had my fill. So here goes . . .

Fear Factor

Dr Chris Whitty reads a bedtime story
to one of his younger patients

What to do when you want young children to get back into bed? Tell them the Bogeyman will grab their ankles and gobble them up, one toe at a time. What to do when you need to get the trireme home in time for tea? Ask the Nubian chap on drums to up the beat a little and crack the whip over the slave-deck oarsmen. Fear, as Kenneth Clark knew, is an old weapon. The Romans, scenting mutiny, selected one man in ten from the legion and executed him. Fear is also used in the annual Christmas horror films from the Department of Transport. It devises heart-stopping little shockers – a newly orphaned child clutching her blood-spattered teddy bear – and a stern voiceover tells us not to risk even half a schooner of sherry before driving.

The civil service engaged in the same low game for the Covid pandemic. Our officials may seem watery, hand-wringing souls. They may attend conferences on inclusivity and spend lunchtimes chewing beansprouts from plastic tubs; but behind that façade thump didactic hearts. It just happens to be difficult to goose-step in Lib Dem sandals.

At the start of the plague, the authorities worried about public disobedience. How could they stifle scepticism about lockdown? Answer: frighten the knickers off us. On 22 March 2020, behavioural science sub-group SPI-B of SAGE prepared the paper, 'Options for Increasing Adherence to Social Distancing Measures'. When talking to the public, officials and ministers should stop asking the public to 'try to' do certain things to improve hygiene. They should use the more starkly imperative 'do'. The paper continued: 'Phrases such as "as much as is practicable", "non-essential", "significantly limit", and "gathering" are open to wide differences in interpretation. This can lead to confusion.' Translation: don't give the snivelling cheats any wiggle room. The paper concluded that 'guidance now needs to be reformulated to be behaviourally specific: who needs to do what (precisely)'. You can sense the author piercing the paper as he or she scratched the words on the page. Then comes this humdinger of a paragraph, which I am italicising because it is so astonishing: '*A substantial number of people still do not feel sufficiently personally threatened . . . The perceived level of personal threat needs to be increased among those who are complacent, using hard-hitting emotional messaging.*'

Deeper in the document is a paragraph about how to 'incentivise' citizens to obey authority. 'Social approval' should be manipulated. Give the citizens a handful of Good Boy choc drops every now and again. 'Social approval can be a powerful source of reward. Not only can this be provided directly by highlighting examples of good practice and providing strong social encouragement and approval in communications; members of the community can be encouraged to provide it to each other. This can have a beneficial spill-over effect of promoting social cohesion.' If we still did not obey, we would have to be scolded. 'Social disapproval from one's community can play an important role in preventing anti-social behaviour or discouraging failure to enact pro-social behaviour. It needs to be accompanied by clear messaging and promotion of strong collective identity. Consideration should be given to use of social disapproval.'

There you have it, ladies and gentlemen. Big government was waving the stick. It was setting us against one another and telling us off, even as the prime minister was saying he would 'put an arm' round us all.

Basil Fawlty Lives

They do things by the book at Crownhill Crematorium, Milton Keynes. By 'the book' one does not mean the Bible or Torah or Koran. Goodness me, no. Modern officialdom is suspicious of religious texts. Milton Keynes council stresses that its crematorium is on 'dedicated, rather than consecrated' ground. The 'book' I refer to is the set of regulations that govern the conduct of funerals. If you break them you will find yourself on a bed of hot coals.

An autumn day in 2020 saw the funeral of Alan Wright, a local man. Arrangements were made for this doleful occasion to be conducted at the Crownhill Crem. Mr Wright's family and friends duly gathered. Promotional material about the Crownhill celebrates its 'undulating and attractive grounds', the planting of the trees reflecting 'a woodland design'. Mourners, lifting their misty gaze to this vista, may be comforted by the timelessness of Mother Nature's bounty, the gambol of squirrels, the susurration of a breeze through the branches and the chatter of calming birdsong. Inside, the crem offers 'up-to-date features' and a chapel of remembrance with a flower-lined 'porte-cochère'. The place has been designed 'to impart an air of serenity and simplicity'. A range of poems and readings, including an inexplicably large number of American-Indian verses, is suggested to grieving families. Electric organ music vibrates in the air, soft enough to stroke the melancholy soul yet strong enough to cover the weeping as families arrive and leave.

Mr Wright's funeral was held at a time of social-distancing measures. Mourners were shown to individual chairs set well apart from each other. At funerals it may be said that we huddle before our destinies, stooping in the shadow of death. At such moments the firmest faith is confronted. The funeral's officiant opened the service by saying it was an honour to be taking the funeral. At this point Mr Wright's widow, quite naturally, started to crumple. If you had been there and had been her son seated six feet to the right, what would you have done? You would, I suggest, have moved your chair and gone to hold her hand. This is what happened. Another man moved his seat, so that Mrs Wright was propped up on either side. The officiant was just saying the words 'as we unite in love and friendship' when there came an interruption from the back of the room. A crematorium attendant had seen the chair movers and he was not pleased. Not pleased at all. By comforting Mrs Wright, the two men had broken the social-distance requirements. Were they crazy? The attendant burst in on the service, holding wide his arms and saying, 'You'll have to put the chairs back, I'm afraid. You can't move the chairs.' The mourners obeyed in silence. The attendant walked back to his guard post, taking a triumphant look over his right shoulder to make sure they were not playing silly-buggers the moment he returned to his control tower.

Mrs Wright's son later told the *Milton Keynes Citizen* that he had been in his mother's support bubble for weeks. 'I can sit in a restaurant, I can sit in a pub, I can live at my mother's house, I can travel in a limousine to the crematorium with six people, but when I want to give my mum a hug at Dad's funeral, a man flies out mid-service shouting stop the service and makes us split. It scared my daughter and shocked everyone in the room. It was a devastating day made even worse. This is not how funerals should be.' At which the jobsworth will retort that in fact it *is* how funerals should be, thank you, because we say so in the rules.

They seem to go in for this sort of behaviour in Northamptonshire, where traffic wardens slapped a parking ticket on the windscreen of a hearse as it was waiting to be loaded with a coffin. Something similar happened in 2003 to a hearse at Leith, near Edinburgh. A council spokesman said: 'The parking attendant observed that there was no activity around the vehicle.' Nor much inside it, presumably.

Bossiness – a Brief History

For all we know, it began one evening a few score millennia ago. Neanderthal Man was outside his cave, preparing dinner, when up sauntered a neighbour who glared at the barbecue and said: 'Residential zone, mate. You got approval for that fire? You're filling other caves with the smell of charred mammoth and the vegetarians among us find that frankly unacceptable.' Nor can it have been easy being Zipporah, wife of Moses. There went a husband with firm opinions. Do this, don't do that, yadda yadda yadda, all topped by those timeless and deadly words: 'I have it on good authority.' The moment was lost to Kodak but we can imagine Gershom and Eliezer rolled their eyes when Moses blew in from Mount Sinai. 'Uh-oh, Dad's in one of his bossy moods again.' Zipporah will have known what it was to be ground down by instructions. Sometimes she must have wished her dear beloved would go and jump in a lake. Mind you, he'd then probably only go and divide it.

There have been megalomaniacs down the ages. They were usually more honest about it. Despots took a pride in dynamic assertion. 'To be a king is half to be a god,' cries Tamburlaine in Christopher Marlowe's account of

13

that troublesome Turco-Mongol conqueror who used his defeated rival Bazajeth as a footstool. Today's arm lifters go about things more subtly. They wrap us in their moist considerations. They use Aussie-Californian uplift. They say 'so' at the start of their sentences and with a pitying smile ask us if we have any questions. We do. Just the one: 'Why won't you leave us alone?'

Ebenezer Scrooge is sometimes held up as the antonym to Christmas joy but compared to Oliver Cromwell, Scrooge was a gay goose. Cromwell (Lib Dem, Huntingdonshire) was Lord Protector of the Commonwealth of England, Scotland and Ireland from 1653 to 1658. He felt that Christmas revelry had nothing to do with Christianity. And so he and his political movement banned it. Troops were ordered to patrol the streets of London, ensuring that shops remained open and that no celebrations were being held. As soon as glum-bucket Oliver was in his box and Charles II was on the throne, Christmas was un-banned and the carousing recommenced. But whose statue stands outside the House of Commons? Cromwell's. The man who banned fun. How appropriate.

A. Hitler, B. Mussolini and J. V. Stalin were foot-stamping maniacs who liked to throw their weight around. Roman emperors were self-consciously imperious. All those insistently straight roads suggest an early tendency to OCD. The Normans were severe with their brutalising castles, flat-nosed helmets and the centralised bureaucracy of the Domesday Book, an explosion of red tape from which England has never quite recovered. This island, before the Normans, was a kingdom of bucolic

Old Ironpants: Christmas bunting not his thing

freedoms, dappled glades and tinkling brooks, a place
where young bloods blew on yew horns, the Anglo-Saxon
owned his land, and mead-supping monks spent happy
weeks gilt-filling the Os on their manuscripts. Something
like that, anyway. Under William the Conqueror, life
changed – much of it to pay the new king's military
expenses. Fines went to official courts rather than as
compensation to victims. The words prison, agreement,
justice, court, constable, debt, evidence and justice were
introduced. A net was being spread. When you receive
your modern tax return, you can blame William of
Normandy. When you are fined £200 for not wearing a
mask, blame William. When you receive a summons for
so much as touching your mobile telephone in a traffic
jam, blame the law-obsessed Normans.

Tax, which took off after the Domesday Book, has
become the favourite weapon of bossy politicians. By

whacking up the price of something the people enjoy – tobacco, dry sack, malt, even windows – they aim to control us and fill the state's coffers. There have been rebellions. Nicholas Vansittart, Chancellor of the Exchequer 1812–1823, tried to keep income tax in place after the Battle of Waterloo, but parliament could not bear the idea. It was scrapped with 'a thundering peal of applause' and the Commons ruled that all documents associated with income tax should be 'collected, cut into pieces and pulped'. The tax returned. Of course it did. And they invented ever more ways to take and spend our money. Now we are in such debt that we will never shake off their parasitic pestilence. As for Vansittart, Canning noted his 'pious and demure' appearance and the fact that he was a notorious mumbler. Couldn't spit out the words clearly. He was one of those timorous despots who plague us to this day.

Henry VIII could be annoyingly single-minded but at least he told Rome to get stuffed. The Enclosure Acts and Highland Clearances were examples of government buggeration and bureaucratic encroachment. In the nineteenth century, bossiness was the work of social convention, with table legs covered to stem lustful thoughts. A century later there was the pointless collection of scrap metal in World War Two, ordered because it was 'needed for the war effort' whereas it was simply done to create 'social cohesion' (as SAGE calls it). Same with rules on blackouts and carrying gas masks. They were almost completely pointless in terms of saving lives. The propelling motive, always, was nanny, nanny, nanny. You will say, 'We love Mary Poppins.' The point about Ms Poppins was that she was the only good nanny. The rest were bullies.

As we tramp through life's tribulations, hectored one way, harassed the other, as habeas corpus laws are flattened by a power-drunk government, as we are buffeted hither and thither by regulations and conventions and expectations and best-practice guidelines and risk-management routines and standardisations and accounting procedures, our example must be the seventeenth-century mathematician and astronomer Galileo Galilei. The Vatican did not like Galileo's attitude. He was saying things that challenged religious orthodoxy about the stars. He was prosecuted and his books were banned. It was an early example of cancel culture. The Pope's cronies extracted a meaningless retraction from him. Pure Hollywood 2020. Galileo knew that our world revolved around the sun but he caved in to their allegations of heresy. He was placed under house arrest. He was told to read the penitential psalms in an almost never-ending sequence. The papal authorities said this would improve him, just as a modern 'speed-awareness course' or 'unconscious-bias training' will re-programme errant motorists and corporate foot soldiers. Maybe Galileo's agent advised him to retract his beliefs as a career-saving move. Anything for a quiet life, mate. But in his heart Galileo held fast to his beliefs. He knew he was right. '*E pur si muove*,' he growled. Earth *did* move, and no end of bossiness would change that.

My friend Tom, done for speeding, took the option of attending a speed-awareness course rather than accept points on his licence. He found it less than riveting. At the end he asked the instructors: 'If I get done again for speeding, do I get my money back?' They didn't like that.

Bans Bomb

Carveries, Klackers, *Little Britain*, TikTok, foie gras, junk food ads, energy drinks, ivory, *The Life of Brian*, juke-boxes, *Lady Chatterley's Lover*, hunting, blowing a trombone or trumpet, nail bars, tattooing, the Robertson's golliwog, teaching children about gay love, bedding your neighbour, beauty parlours, babysitters, beauty spots, broadcasting Irish Republican voices, *The Black and White Minstrel Show*, cotton buds, *The Human Centipede 2*, drinks parties in Bolton, dirty weekends in Barcelona, outdoor heaters, indoor theatres, Diwali, drinking straws: all have been subject to bans. Some, such as the censoring of *The Human Centipede 2*, may be understandable for reasons of sheer critical horror, others for self-preservation – Klacker toys had a tendency to shatter, shards of plastic flying towards children's eyes. But many of these bans were driven by bossiness, a desire to stop other people having fun. Killjoy woz 'ere.

Personally, I do not care about TikTok, whatever it might be. Beauty parlours and nail bars are to me a foreign realm, I can't abide D. H. Lawrence and my neighbours' virtue was safe even before Boris Johnson – of all people – ruled that bonking anyone from outside your immediate household was a no-no. But personal preference has nothing to do with it. Bans raise a point of principle. The bonking ban was what did it for Neil Ferguson, epidemiologist and, as it turned out, enthusiastic skinny-wriggler. Ferguson was the SAGE committee member whose wild overestimate of likely Covid deaths panicked the government into Lockdown 1. His work was not peer-reviewed because he was strangely coy about his figures. Less coy about whipping off his smalls and hopping into bed with another chap's wife, though. Prof. Lockdown became Prof. Pantsdown. That did not stop the BBC using him as a pandemic pundit. Ferguson was pro big-state and pro big-science. He was also anti-Brexit, oozed metropolitan snootiness, was scruffy and obviously a *Guardian* reader. Get him on the box. Dominic Cummings, the Svengali of 10 Downing Street, went whizzing off to Co. Durham when he had the virus, even while forcing the rest of the country to 'stay at home and save lives'. Margaret Ferrier MP, of the Scots Nats, was soon hurtling in the other direction, Glasgow to London, while awaiting the result of a Covid test. Told that she was indeed infected, she jumped on a train back home. Laws? We make them, my dear. We don't follow them. And then came the unzipping of hands-on Hancock, the man who told us not to mingle but then played tonsil-hockey with his sultry adviser. Hands, face, tongue, swabs, swoon.

Who could blame the Panstdowns, Cummingses and Ferriers? They had spotted that bans are a waste of time. Bans bomb. Bans make their proponents feel big but are frequently pointless. In 1988 Margaret Thatcher acted to stop the Irish Republicans from receiving 'the oxygen of publicity'. She said their voices could no longer be broadcast. Broadcasters got round this by having actors dub the voices of Gerry Adams and co. The IRA and their ilk were murderous thugs and Mrs Thatcher had good reason to dislike them. But her ban, which lasted until 1994, just made the government look petty and heavy-handed. It created *more* publicity for the terrorists, not less.

Do as I say: take yer knickers off

The 2004 fox-hunting ban, if viewed as a move against animal suffering – which was certainly how it was presented – was similarly questionable. What is good for foxes is almost certainly bad for lambs and chickens. Before the ban, hunting was not much of a thing round our way. Since the ban, it has acquired the cachet of cultural resistance. The ban made heroes of hunt masters and the police have allowed hunting to continue, provided hounds only follow dragged scents. Of course they do.

The ban, more honestly, was an act of political spite against Barbour-wearers.

As a child growing up in the 1960s, I was mad about cowboys. Milky-Bar-Kid-style, I'd dress up in a cowboy hat and a fake-leather waistcoat, just like Trampas in *The Virginian*. I had two cap revolvers, a cap rifle and a pop gun. I'd twiddle the revolvers on my index fingers. Wyatt Earp would have been impressed. My toy rifle had barrel mouldings to replicate a proper gun. The firing mechanism allowed a spool of caps to turn with each shot and the little explosions left a pleasing smell of Armstrong's explosive mixture. The gun sometimes jammed, but then so did John Wayne's rifle in the Sunday afternoon films, normally at some crucial moment when he was doing battle with Red Indians. We were allowed to say Red Indian in those days. Not that they were red. Like everything else on our nursery telly, they were black and white. For my fifth birthday I was given a Captain Scarlet playsuit. Captain Scarlet was a children's TV character who protected Earth from the Mysterons, and it was just as well he did, because few other grown-ups of my acquaintance seemed to take the Mysterons seriously. The playsuit contained a lot of foam which was itchy and smelled of cheap glue. The peaked cap was okay, though, and there was a futuristic gun which one could whip out of one's pocket and shoot round corners. Bang-bang, you're dead, I'm not. Today, toy guns are seldom seen. Replica firearms have been banned and children are encouraged to play with less 'dangerous' toys. Some nurseries will not even admit children who are wearing superhero costumes because they may have unhealthy ideas about defending themselves and fighting evil.

How mass killers start

In 2018, Prince George, aged four, was seen playing with a toy gun at a polo match in Tetbury. Up went the Greek chorus on social media, busybodies saying how 'disappointing' it was that Kate and William allowed their child to normalise firearms. The *Daily Mirror* reported 'outrage' at the photograph. The gun was a water pistol which had been won at a children's funfair. In its first sentence, the *Mirror* linked the snaps of Prince George to 'a surge in violence in the UK', as though George was part of that crime wave, or responsible for inciting it. The National Union of Teachers has claimed that pop guns can 'symbolise aggression'. What droning miseries. It's enough to make you want to reach for your spud gun (I had one of those, too) and propel a fast-hurtling pellet of potato at the nearest teaching union leader. Aim for the cheek. Stings like jiminy.

The case against toy guns is that they glamorise and normalise. After the Dunblane murders, when an armed maniac shot dead sixteen children and one teacher, there was a swing of opinion against handguns. A vicar in Berkshire organised an 'amnesty' for toy guns. Local children were instructed to hand in any pop guns or cap guns or cowboy guns and they would escape punishment, even though such toys were not illegal. The Rev. John Harper said: 'It is good to stimulate thinking in the minds of children about what weapons can do and whether it is good to play with pretend weapons.' Pamela Orpinas, an American public-health professor, claimed that children who played with toy guns were more likely to become aggressive in adulthood. 'Children should be taught to resolve conflict through peaceful means,' she said. 'We must make them aware that weapons are not acceptable – and that includes toy ones.' Raising awareness: it is a favoured phrase of the bossocracy. And it never stops. A child cannot say, 'Thanks, I'm aware of that, now stop lecturing me.' Bossocrats will say they need to be made *more* aware. Purity, like the rainbow's pot of gold, is always out of reach.

The Blair government banned beef on the bone in 1997 in response to mad cow disease. T-bone steaks became harder to buy than cocaine. It was two years before the chief medical officer, Liam Donaldson, said the risk was 'tiny and unquantifiable', and another three months before sales could resume. Officaldom hates to surrender a nice juicy ban. In 1998 we went to a party at the house of a JP near Tetbury. He served the most deliciously pink beef on the bone and disclosed that he was the main 'dealer' for central Gloucestershire. Did any of us wish to place an order? Pointless rules make outlaws even of magistrates.

Driving Us to Drink

Colleagues of Dame Sally Davies voice
hopes for an office Christmas party

One of many depressing things about the Great
Depression in America was that the sale and importa-
tion of intoxicating liquor was illegal there at the time.
The eighteenth amendment to the US constitution held
sway from 1920 to 1933. Strong drink was banned.

Americans who lost fortunes in the stock market crash of late 1929 therefore could not legally glug a consoling bottle of Jim Beam. They may have jumped to their deaths from Wall Street's skyscrapers but at least they had clean livers.

Outwardly, all was proper. The anti-drink lobby got its amendment on to the US constitution, politicians said the law would be enforced and the feds regularly swooped. Temperance campaigners wore their 'Fight for Right' badges and presidential candidates, impressed by this vehement rectitude, sought the backing of the Anti-Saloon League. Twenties America was ostensibly as dry as twenty-first-century Riyadh. And yet, and yet . . . the common herd refused to obey. Americans carried on boozing. In 1920, just before the ban began, there were 1,700 bars in Philadelphia. Thirteen years later, 1,200 were still in business. For every bar that was closed, six speakeasies opened. Cheers!

This public dissent enraged those in authority. Officials hate it when the public ignores rules. Remember Bournemouth beach in July 2020? Packed. 'You'll all catch Covid,' wailed the health maniacs. No spike in infections occurred. Officials in Prohibition America took vicious action against the rule breakers. They 'denatured' – i.e., poisoned – the raw alcohol used by bootleggers. People who drank it died. That'll learn 'em. The Anti-Saloon League shrugged that drinkers were simply committing suicide. Wayne Bidwell Wheeler, the attorney behind the Anti-Saloon League, said 'to root out a bad habit costs many lives'. As many as 50,000 died that way. Wayne Wheeler felt he could live with that figure.

Wheeler was an early proponent of single-issue politics or 'pressure politics'. He achieved the sort of institutional capture not repeated until the early twenty-first century by race-grievance groups and trans-rights hardliners. Wheeler forced his message through schools. The media knelt before him. Public and professional bodies supported him. He was a moralising monster and the establishment lacked the guts to tell him to get lost. Wheeler used his league's baleful, vociferous influence to traduce politicians who resisted his campaign. He ousted the Republican governor of Ohio who, though broadly sympathetic to temperance, thought it might be sensible to compromise with drinkers. Compromise? Be gone, heretic! Today's single-issue crazies use the same moral terrorism. Look at the way J. K. Rowling was trashed by the Left and columnist Suzanne Moore driven out of the *Guardian* after the two of them took a perfectly reasonable position on the language of trans-sexualism. Today's trans ultras would have found kindred spirits in the Anti-Saloon League, though one fancies Wayne B. Wheeler might have run a mile from the Bombshell Club off Leicester Square.

Prohibition gave officials clout and offered opportunities for bribery. Gangsters made fortunes from smuggling. The populace, gasping for a snifter, became blasé about breaking the rules. Respect for the law declined. Mind you, church attendance became popular because communion wine was still permitted. It must have been a job wrenching the chalice out of some hands.

Prohibition had supporters in Britain. In November 1922, Edwin Scrymgeour was elected MP for Dundee.

Scrymgeour belonged to the Scottish Prohibition Party (his campaign slogan: 'Vote for Scrymgeour and Death to the Drink!'). The man he ousted was a certain Winston Churchill. Scrymgeour served until 1931 and later became a preacher. He died aged 80 in 1947. Churchill, less well known for abstinence, went on to become the statesman of the century. He died in 1965, at 90 per cent proof.

The spirit, if we can call it that, of Scrymgeour has not disappeared. Chris Whitty's predecessor as chief medical officer, Dame Sally Davies, was frightfully bossy when it came to the drink. She said every time we reached for a toot we should bear in mind the health damage. Make their flesh creep, Sally! Get the old fear factor going. 'Do as I do,' she said in her prissy tones, 'and when I reach for my glass of wine, think "do I want my glass of wine or do I want to raise my risk of breast cancer?". I take a decision each time.' Photographs of Dame Sally with a glass of plonk to hand are not unknown. It seems she has often, in response to her own question, decided that the answer is 'Top her up, Luigi.'

Maybe she is right to do so, because official guidance on drinking is flaky. In 1987 a working party at the Royal College of Physicians came up with the number of 'units' we should drink a week (twenty-one for men, fourteen for women). Richard Smith, a member of that group, later admitted that the figures were prompted by 'a feeling that you had to say something'. In 2007 *The Times* reported Mr Smith's admission that it was 'impossible to say what's safe and what isn't'. The report continued:

> *Mr Smith, a former Editor of the British Medical Journal,*
> *said members of the working party were so concerned by*

*growing evidence of the chronic damage caused by heavy,
long-term drinking that they felt obliged to produce guidelines. 'Those limits were really plucked out of the air. They
were not based on any firm evidence at all. It was a sort of
intelligent guess by a committee,' he said.*

Richard Smith is the brother of comedian Arthur
Smith. No further questions, m'lud.

Dame Sally, naturally, thought those invented recommendations far too high, and reduced men's permissible
units so that they were the same as women's. How egali-
tarian of her. She first claimed it was 'an old wives' tale'
that moderate drinking could do you good. At a select
committee she later conceded that some research did
suggest light drinking could be beneficial – one study
even found that a bottle of wine a day would give you
about the same risk of death as a teetotaller. You might
get hiccups more often, though.

During the Covid pandemic, public health zealots had
a chance to impose drinking prohibitions on a Merrie
England that, damn its eyes, had voted to leave the EU
and was insufficiently worshipful about climate change.
'The science' was now in charge and it was going to exact
some revenge. By the way, Dame Sally hated being called
'nanny in chief'. She claimed it was 'sexist'. What? Like
'old wives' tale'?

For all the lectures from medics, we continue to booze
like Vikings. The country plainly has less in common
with Dame Sally Davies than it does with Henry
Youngman, who said, 'When I read about the evils of
drinking, I gave up reading.'

When the top bureaucrat at your leading university tells scholars what to think, you're in trouble. Stephen Toope is vice-chancellor – a title roughly comparable to chief executive – of Cambridge University. This Toope, a Canadian with a background in human rights and public international law, tried to force down Cambridge's gullet a contractual requirement that academics and students 'be respectful of the diverse identities of others'. The logic of this was that savages who practise female genital mutilation would thus have to be 'respected'. Terrorist groups, drug culture, religions that demean women and kill animals with needless cruelty: all would need respecting. Under Toope's ruling, it might even be compulsory to say that you respect Lib Dems. Sir, you push us too far!

Heroically, there was a rebellion. It was led by an atheist don at Caius, Arif Ahmed, who doubted that he would be allowed to discuss the Charlie Hebdo cartoon controversy with undergraduates under Toope's rule. Stephen Fry, actor and writer, added that if someone pointed a gun at his head and demanded respect, 'I could not with any honesty offer it'. Demanding respect with menaces: this is exactly how many single-issue lobbies operate. Ahmed and Fry did us all a service by standing up to Toope but you wonder if the campaign would have succeeded had it been led by intellectuals from less fashionable quarters.

Ahmed proposed that 'respect' should be changed to 'tolerate'. Personally, I wouldn't even have offered that but it was worth doing to defeat Toope's proposal. Defeated it duly was in a (secret) ballot of Cambridge dons. The vice-chancellor, who is paid £475,000 a year, claimed afterwards that it had been a victory for free speech. Indeed it was, but no thanks to him.

Hairy Mary

Mary Whitehouse: the name raises smirks in fashionable circles. Mrs Whitehouse was the satire-proof battleaxe who in 1965 founded the National Viewers' and Listeners' Association, a pressure group that complained about 'filth' on the airwaves. She disliked bad language. She disapproved of on-screen sex. She even objected to a reshowing of Richard Dimbleby's documentary about Belsen. With her hats and eagle-winged spectacles, Mrs Whitehouse pecked at generations of BBC producers and controllers. Her argument was that broadcasting scenes of violence and cruelty and lust normalised those things and left a damaging impression on susceptible minds.

Precisely the same argument is used by illiberal Leftists who want to ban children from using toy guns. We can call this the Mary Whitehouse paradox. The sort of Righties who suspect that sex education in schools is dodgy and serves only to awaken steamy thoughts in young minds may sometimes also think toy guns are harmless. The Lefties who think Mrs Whitehouse was barking mad in her complaints about bad language may sometimes also complain that golliwogs on jam pots could trigger kids into a chorus of the *Horst-Wessel-Lied*. Those who laughed at Mrs Whitehouse's attempt to ban *Romans in Britain* are probably quite often happy to accept that Punch & Judy shows could encourage domestic violence.

She'd have liked the Guardian

In her day, Mrs Whitehouse was a genuine threat to free speech. In 1977 she won a blasphemy case against *Gay News*, which had published a homo-erotic poem about Jesus. The editor of *Gay News*, Denis Lemon, was given a suspended prison sentence. There will be people who approved of that verdict who were appalled by the fatwa against Salman Rushdie twelve years later. If Mary Whitehouse had kept quiet about *Gay News*, hardly anyone would have read that poem about Jesus. If the Ayatollah Khomeini had let Rushdie's *Satanic Verses* go through to the wicketkeeper, it would have sunk into obscurity. Bans really are stupid.

Mrs Whitehouse is usually portrayed as a right-wing figure, but with the years she has become just as much a prophet of the *Guardian*-reading, ban-embracing Left. Mary Whitehouse and Owen Jones: sisters.

No sex please, we're British? Hardly. Sex education is now compulsory in schools and some companies are making a lot of money out of it – a great deal more than the pimps off Leicester Square ever did. The theory is that if you tell children about the birds and the bees, they (the children) will be 'safer'. All schools, from primaries upwards, are now obliged to give relationship and sex education to pupils. They duly spend large sums on sex talkers. Whooppee. Take Big Talk Education, whose logo is a couple of love-heart sweeties. Big Talk's 'team' has twelve women and one man (Dave) and they all wear blue T-shirts. The website shows a class of what look like six year-olds pointing in wonder at a picture being held in front of them by one of the team. You dread to think what it depicted. Big Talk has contracts with schools and pupil referral units up and down England. Products even include a one-day course of statutory relationship education for Gypsy, Roma and Traveller children. One day? Catch them while you can.

Compulsory sex education has been good not only for private companies such as Big Talk but also for proselytising sex-rights charities such as The Proud Trust in Manchester. It campaigns for 'trans positivism' and sees phobia under every stone. The Proud Trust, which pockets enormous sums of public money, goes into primary schools to tell kiddies all about their trans rights. It uses 'toolkits' to tell children about these things. The very mention of 'tool' must set off a certain amount of sniggering from older pupils. Among those tools is a dice game in which the six faces of each die carry one of the following words: vulva, penis, anus, mouth, hands/fingers, object. You shake your two dice and see what comes up. Then you have a discussion with your classmates about how the two upright words can be matched to one another in sexual activity. 'Object' is not specified but it could be anything from a sink plunger to a bottle top. Proud Trust tutors are told not to pass judgement. People who talked about such things in front of children would once have been questioned by police. Now the law is swinging on the other boot, and you will be in trouble with the authorities if you refuse to let your child sit through such sessions.

Dabblers in Politick

This is going to hurt

Whitty and Vallance: the Brothers Grim; Glum and Glummer; the gruesome twosome. Chris Whitty and Sir Patrick Vallance, barely known in February 2020, were by the end of the year established as heralds of misery. The sound of their voices was enough to make Brits punch their sofas. It was not the fault of the two gents themselves. They had a rotten duty to perform. Their fate

– being resented by their fellow countrymen – was nothing personal. It was bigger than that. There was now a sullen loathing of pessimistic data-bods. It was, unfortunately, a hatred of experts.

Michael Gove was Lord Chancellor when in 2016 he shrugged about the IFS, NHS, CBI and TUC being anti-Brexit. Gove: 'I think the people of this country have had enough of experts with organisations with acronyms saying that they know what is best and getting it consistently wrong.' Magnificoes of Remain clutched their necks as if taking part in a national self-throttling contest. How could the Lord Chancellor – the *Lord Chancellor* – attack expertise? Economists and scientists and lawyers had spent years gaining letters after their names. Qualifications brought them money and status. It had been that way since the white-kilt class ran ancient Egypt under the pharaohs. Four years later, the same Gove was Chancellor of the Duchy of Lancaster and Covid had struck. Whitehall's response was steered by the Scientific Advisory Group for Emergencies (SAGE). Few were more worshipful of SAGE than ... Michael Gove. What political elasticity he has.

It is only human to resent know-alls: the swot who begins every intervention with 'actually'; the office nerd who says 'yes, but I think you'll find it's more complicated than that ...' Accomplished in their chosen field though they be, experts are not always savvy. When giving advice on a matter as combustive as a national lockdown, they needed to tread carefully. If they could not see this, they couldn't be so sage.

Chris Whitty and Sir Patrick Vallance went down fine

when they first appeared alongside the prime minister. They seemed to take some of the partisanship out of the crisis. At this point we did not even know the names of SAGE's numerous members, that information being secret. Lean, pale Whitty, the chief medical officer, had a drainpipe neck and gulpy eyes. He only needed a white coat to complete the stereotype of an overworked clap doctor. Vallance, chief scientific adviser, was better tailored, with, you somehow felt, less of a smell of hospital pee about him. As a presentational duo, Whitty and Vallance worked.

Things began to go wrong when another member of SAGE, our friend Neil Ferguson, started to push his chops around the media. Ferguson became a favourite of the Left. SAGE members more sceptical of the lockdown started popping up as favourites of the Right. This was great for the scientists involved. It made them famous and increased their value for future books and TV bookings. It was less good for the Whitehall idea of 'science'. Expertise was being politicised, just as it had been in the Brexit row when economists and trade bodies had blatant agendas. When Ferguson came up with a startling estimate of 500,000 British deaths from Covid, his media friends gave it big play. The government felt obliged to shut businesses and tell us to stay at home. Ferguson seemed to revel in the publicity. At the start of April 2020, he let it be known that he 'hadn't really had a day off since mid-January'. Was that the smell of burning martyr? Then he himself contracted Covid and, naturally, took to Twitter to announce the news. Our hero! He had been standing close to Matt Hancock just a day or so earlier and, in rapid course, both Boris Johnson and Hancock went down with the disease, Johnson being lucky to survive. Ferguson, so fastidious about telling the rest of the country to observe social distancing, may have been the spreader. He certainly wasn't much good at keeping his hands clean. It was in May that word broke he was having a friend over to his house for adulterous gymnastics. He resigned from SAGE but that was not the last we heard of him. He had become a symbol not of scientific rigour but of one side of the story.

A few other coronavirus experts now started to fancy themselves media celebs: Spiegelhalter, Rubin, Semple, Sikora, Shattock, Prof. Tom Cobbleigh and all. Who can blame them? Government funding of academic institutions is awarded, in part, on media coverage. If that also brings lucrative publishing and punditry opportunities for the individual, well, yippee. Other SAGE members beside Whitty and Vallance co-starred at the Downing Street press conferences. Some were terrible. Some, such as Jonathan Van-Tam, plainly lapped up the exposure and performed like sea lions at Bristol Zoo. None of this was doing public trust in science much good. Oxford's Prof. Carl Heneghan co-wrote a *Spectator* article about a Danish study which appeared to show that masks were pretty much a waste of time. The establishment was appalled. For God's sake, you can't go telling the plebs that we have been lying to them. Look at all the trouble we went to in order to create fear! Facebook duly censored the article, saying that its 'independent fact checkers' knew better than the director of Oxford University's Centre for Evidence-Based Medicine. Back at

SAGE, Prof. John Edmunds made such a name for himself as a Covid pessimist that he became known as 'Prof. Scrooge'. His colleague, Sir Venki Ramakrishnan, argued that not wearing a mask should become as great a taboo as drink-driving. Sir Venki was president of the Royal Society, which presumably believes in evidence-based science.

> I have been dubious about scientists since school, when doing a biology practical at O level and we were told to measure the breathing rate of a locust which had been jammed into a tube. My tube had been sealed with a large pink rubber bung. I signalled to our teacher that there was a problem. He wafted me away, indicating that this was an exam setting and I should continue unassisted. But how could I measure the breathing rate? My locust was dead. Suffocated. Murdered. By science!

Even if you did not accept that Danish study, the evidence supporting masks was wobbly. Why would the president of the Royal Society make such a trenchant claim? Remember the paper mentioned at the start of this book, the one that wanted to created social disapproval? Sir Venki Rampitup-Krishnan was busy earning his little knighthood.

Another SAGE member whipping up the ante was Sir Jeremy Farrar, a busy member of the Twittersphere. He enjoys reposting complimentary Tweets about himself. There's a word for that sort of self-gratifier and it isn't 'scientist'. Sir Jeremy's Tweets did not mention his income. In 2019 he was paid £524,537 to be director of the

Wellcome Trust, which exists to support public under-standing of science. Sir Jeremy has held the Wellcome job since 2013 and his 2019 money was a sharp rise (though not quite exponential, to use a popular phrase) on the £455,761 he bagged in 2018. It is quite a charity – yes, charity, with all the attendant tax perks – that pays such riches. The trustees of the Wellcome Trust do all right for themselves, too. Lady Manningham-Buller, the former MI5 boss who chairs it, received £142,108 in 2019. Ker-bloody-ching! And she only read English at univer-sity. The Trust's fourteen governors were paid a total of £627,644. Never let it be said that the science charity sector does not look after its front-line workers. And yet there, on SAGE, was Farrar the half-a-million-a-year man demanding a lockdown which would hit the poorest hardest. He agitated for it. He attacked sceptics. He supported Neil Ferguson. Give that knight of the realm some pom-poms and a short skirt and a dental brace.

At Downing Street, Whitty and Vallance were starting to lose their early shine. The public was becoming weary of their pessimism and their graphs. Public health advo-cates seldom measured lockdown in the wider context of the economic damage and other health problems it caused. There were accusations that Vallance and Whitty were using out-of-date statistics and exaggerating dangers and rolling Boris towards more national lockdowns in England. The one-time objective science bods were being seen as partisan. It might have been better for 'the science' if they had not been exposed to public attention on such a regular basis. Yet Boris Johnson and Matt Hancock – and Michael Gove – wanted their expertise to frighten the public into accepting the loss of liberties. Science had become the gaolers' accomplice.

One of Vallance's predecessors, Sir David King, still itchy for attention, started a rival to SAGE. This was called 'Independent SAGE'. King, tarting himself round the media, said he started his group because Dominic Cummings was leaning on the real SAGE to be anti-lockdown. It turned out that Cummings was actually a supporter of lockdown. Sir David won himself airtime at the start of his enterprise – that may have been the chief intention all along – but his alternative SAGE failed to gain sustained media traction. The idea SAGE was defer-ring to ministers was clearly bonkers. It was the other way round. As for King's 'independent' committee, ten of its twelve members had a record of being anti-Tory or anti-Boris. They included two communists, two former Labour Party donors, one Momentum enthusiast and eight who backed Jeremy Corbyn in the 2019 general election. James Boswell once called Samuel Johnson a 'dabbler in physick'. Did we now have dabblers in politick?

The Wellcome Trust's desire for greater public under-standing of science was being fulfilled in an unexpected way: we understood that they were as vain and flawed and disputative as the rest of us. 'Following the science' was, to use a laboratory term, bollocks.

Could someone maybe start a charity which seeks to promote greater scientific understanding of the public?

Coin Con

Black History Month was looming again and Whitehall's finest were in a panic. If they failed to do something special they would be accused of racism. 'I know,' said a bright spark at the Treasury. 'Let's strike a commemorative coin.' Thus, on 17 October 2020, a 'Diversity Built Britain' 50p bit was produced. The PM said: 'It echoes the government's commitment to building a fairer society for all.' The Chancellor held a 'round table' with its designer and campaigners. 'Education packs' were sent to primary schools and Whitehall Twitter streams filled with the exciting news. The head of the Royal Mint called it 'one of the most significant coins' ever produced in Britain. 'This marks the beginning of a new chapter.' It was nothing less than a 'pivotal' 50p.

It made a 'news in brief' paragraph in one of the papers.

Ethics Man

Experts have undermined the idea of expertise not just by parading themselves as media pundits but also by appeasing politicised grievance culture with codes of conduct. A major culprit in this has been that nuisance Sir David King.

When you cross a bridge, which worries you more: that the bridge stays in one piece until you are on the other side, or that the engineer who built it promoted equality, diversity and inclusion? When you take medicine, which is more important to you: that it soothes your throat or that the chemist who mixed it was committed to social justice?

When Sir David King was chief scientific adviser from 2000 to 2007, he made a fool of himself over diesel cars, as I noted in my v. good book *Patronising Bastards*. We have just seen how he was the guiding genius behind the (not-so) Independent SAGE. Another of his contributions to human progress was the Universal Ethical Code for Scientists, introduced when he was *el grand queso* at 10 Downing Street. This, like other codes of conduct, is an attempt to force professionals to conform to the moral preferences of top people (i.e., Sir David King). The Universal Ethical Code for

Scientists is supervised by Whitehall's Department for Business, or Lambeth Palace, as it is not known. The department dishes out taxpayers' money to scientists. That creates financial leverage: sign up to our moral code or your funding could evaporate. Very ethical!

King explained that his code was about 'our social licence to act as scientists'. His word 'licence' is telling. At its core, science is the acquiring of knowledge. Knowledge should not require 'licence' from government bureaucrats. Licence is another way of saying 'permission'. Knowledge is a right. When rights need a licence, they cease to be rights.

Scientific training sharpens scepticism, so one might have expected science bodies to take a wary look at this 'code of ethics' from a government. And yet they swallowed it whole. How biddable the British elite has become. The Royal Astronomical Society told its stargazing members they must 'act with skill and care' at all times. Don't knock yourself out with that swivelling telescope, you blithering clot. The astronomers were also told they must 'maintain up-to-date skills and assist their development in others ... minimise any adverse effect your work may have on animals and the natural environment ... and seek to discuss the issues that science raises for society'. Why should it be any business of an astronomical society whether or not its members 'assist the development of up-to-date skills' in their colleagues? What if those colleagues are arch-enemies? Is scholastic rivalry no longer a useful spur to scientific advance? The phrase 'seek to discuss the issues that science raises' is odd. 'Agree to discuss' might have been one thing. But 'seeking to discuss' makes it an active imperative, a requirement for flappy-trouser-legged, moon-spotting, monocle-popping Patrick Moores to barge into other people's conversations and start 'raising issues that science raises for society'. This is bound to lead to truculent responses. Oh well, if you tell an astronomer to go and stuff his 'issues' some place where the sun don't shine, he should at least have a range of astral locations.

The Royal Academy of Engineering and the Engineering Council are regulators for a quarter of a million engineers. They beat Sir David King to his ethical code by two years, producing a 'statement of ethical principles' in 2005. So far as one can gather, there had not been any particular moral atrocity in the engineering world to spark this Moses-style law-giving. Perhaps they just wanted to tell other people what to do. That sort of thing used to be called bossiness. Nowadays it is dressed up as corporate best practice. Among other things, the statement of ethical principles, updated in 2017, made it a duty for engineers to:

Act in a reliable and trustworthy manner.
Be alert to the ways in which their work and behaviour might affect others and respect the privacy, rights and reputations of other parties and individuals.
Respect confidentiality.
Avoid deception.
Reject bribery and improper influence.
Recognise the importance of physical and cyber security.

Respect the quality of built and natural environments.

Maximise the public good and minimise both actual and potential adverse effects for their own and succeeding generations.

Take due account of the limited availability of natural resources.

Uphold the reputations and standing of the profession.

Keep their knowledge and skills up to date.

Assist the development of engineering skills in others.

Respect reasoned alternative views.

Beware of the issues that technology raises for society and listen to the concerns of others.

Promote equality, diversity and inclusion.

Promote public awareness of the impact and benefits of engineering achievements.

Challenge statements or policies that cause them professional concern.

Why the hell should they? They are engineers, not tonsured cenobites. They are bridge builders and car designers and inventors of lifts and widgets and guns and elasticated bra straps, not builders of the New Jerusalem. What business is it of an engineer in, say, a bathrooms factory in Sedgefield to 'promote equality, diversity and inclusion' or to proselytise about 'the impact and benefits of engineering achievements'? He or she might quite easily hate engineering and be doing it simply to pay the bills until something better comes along. How does 'respecting confidentiality' fit with 'challenging state-ments or policies that cause professional concern'? Is it really the function of an engineer of sports cars, or warplanes, or a production line making cigarettes, to 'maximise the public good' and worry about 'succeeding generations'? This list of ethics is politicised pap.

Recent presidents of the Royal Academy of Engineering have included Lord Browne, one-time chief executive of BP. His crest, commissioned when he became a peer, shows a bittern booming. Should it not have been a dead seagull blackened by an oil slick? Lord Browne is at home in the Russian business world. Remind us: promoting equality and inclusion, taking account of limited natural resources, challenging dodgy behaviour ... He was succeeded as president of the academy by Sir John Parker, who did eight lucrative years chairing the mining company Anglo-American, which extracts sharply limited natural resources from the loins of Mother Africa.

Codes of conduct are just corporate arse-covering, virtue semaphore and feeble compliance to interference by pressure politics. We are being conned into accepting institutions as fountains of worthiness – look at us, we like gay rights and we employ chaps with turbans! – whereas they are no better or worse than the rest of us. Coca-Cola is a fizzy drinks company. Take a bottle of water, add bubbles and stuff, stick a cap on it and sell it to a thirsty public. That's basically the operation. Not great for the teeth or girth but if we choose to make ourselves fat and gummy, that's up to us. Turn to the code-of-conduct web page for Coca-Cola employees and you are assailed by 'policies, practices and reports' on everything from sustainability to workplace rights, anti-bribery, digital media principles, hateful activity policy, political contributions and supplier requirements. It's enough to make you go pop. Can these really be the people who manufacture gazillions of gallons of gut-rotting gunk, or are they a branch office of the Church of England Synod? You might think Starbucks is a place to grab a quick (expensive) coffee. Wrong. Starbucks exists 'to inspire and nurture the human spirit, one person, one cup and one neighbourhood at a time', and its staff and suppliers must sign up to that 'mission' if they wish to continue to be employed. The company's founder, Howard Schultz, prefaces its 'business ethics and compliance' rules with a foreword saying that 'a commitment to integrity, acting honestly and ethically are critical'. Bear that in mind next time you hear how little corporation tax Starbucks has paid, or how it shafts its competitors and stiffs Ethiopian farmers.

At British Aerospace they have ethics helplines to assist any workers who may suddenly be struggling with the rights and wrongs of making high-tech armaments for use in wars. Amid preachy stuff about being responsible and proud and ethical and observing human rights, complete with a photograph of chief executive Charles Woodburn looking like a happy-clappy bishop and other snapshots of spotlessly diverse employees, lies a warning to staff that if they fail to follow the code of conduct they could be given the boot. BAE states its moist commitment to the environment – 'we have a responsibility to minimise the environmental impacts associated with our products'. Its 'product family' happens to include heavy bombs, torpedoes and depth charges, artillery munition, mortar bombs and unspecified goodies for the Royal Navy's nuclear submarines. All beautifully eco-friendly, we can be sure. Even the Arcadia group under that God-fearing, skeletal hermit Sir Philip Green had a code on conduct – pretty short, mind you, being not much more than four sides of loosely spaced A4. One rather respects the Piz-Buined old brute for keeping it short rather than rabbiting on about his ethical standards like some of the other grotesques of Western capitalism. I bet Sir Philip, even after his recent travails, is more fun over dinner than Howard Schultz.

I'm Not Offended

Every defeat is *ignominious* or a *humiliation*. Errors come in *catalogues*. Failure arrives as a *litany* and *FURY* is capitalised, at least by tabloid websites. Behold the hijacking and dilution of offence. Grievance has become an exaggerated cliché and it is almost a civic duty. If you do not proclaim anger or upset, you are letting the side down. That, in turn, could distress 'victims'. And that would make you a bad person.

Protestors who ripped down the statue of Edward Colston in Bristol and dumped him in the dock – splosh! – were reportedly motivated by indignation at a slave trade that ended 200 years ago. The Oxford students who mobilised against Cecil Rhodes on his plinth at Oriel College were fuelled by honest umbrage at his . . . philanthropy. How dare the old pig be so generous? When Dominic Cummings took his drive to Co. Durham, Sir Keir Starmer QC called it 'an insult to the people of Britain' and the *Guardian* found a voter who considered it 'beyond an insult'. Sir Keir, meanwhile, 'took the knee' with his deputy, Angela Rayner, to show solidarity with the Black Lives Matter movement in America. The two of them looked as if they were about to run the 100 yards.

Keir did one of his wary stares – don't you bloody well try pinching one of my sausages – and Angela went for the blow-dried, pink-cardie look. Mother Angelica in a short skirt and bovver boots. It was not long before she was back to her old self, scratching her pits in the Commons and slagging off a Tory MP for being 'scum'. She can be a rough old bint, Angela, and is much better that way. Please, spare us the damp hankies. Not to be outdone, ever-thoughtful grime artist Stormzy accused Boris Johnson of emboldening hate-mongers. Could this be the same Stormzy who made a record, 'Vossi Bop', which contained the line 'f*** the government and f*** Boris'?

On yer marks, get set ... GO!

Anti-capitalist demonstrators once placed a strip of grass on Sir Winston Churchill's head in Parliament Square. It looked like a punk rocker's green Mohican haircut. This was presented as a slur on the memory of

Churchill. The culprit, a student, was sent to prison for thirty days and given a £250 fine. Last time I looked I was not particularly Marxist, but Churchill's grass Mohican made me laugh. Likewise, I loved the climate-change nudists who – to the indignation of the then Speaker – glued their bums to the bullet-proof glass in the House of Commons. That chap who gave Theresa May a 'P45' during her disastrous party conference speech was, I thought, pretty funny, yet commentators grumbled that he had been irresponsible. When Julian Assange, accused of sexual offences, took refuge in the Ecuadorean embassy, snoots declared it a disgrace. Cheer up! The Ecuadorean ambassador, initially excited by the publicity, started tapping his wristwatch after a week or so and asking his guest when he was going to leave. Señor Assange, not remarkable for clean linen, ended up staying seven years. Worse than Queen Mary.

The other evening we watched an episode of Ronnie Barker's *Porridge*. It was that one about the tin of pineapple chunks. Pure, innocent comedy. Yet the website page carried a warning that *Porridge* was a product of its era and we must brace ourselves for the possibility that some of the content might be offensive. You would need to be a very frail bloom to be bruised by anything Ronnie Barker said. At least he wasn't removed from view, as happened to John Cleese in the 'Don't mention the war!' episode of *Fawlty Towers*. That fell foul of claims it was racist. Could the steaming fools not see that the comedy mocked Basil Fawlty, not the Krauts? Oops. Now look and see what you've gone and made me do. Write 100 times, 'I must not call Germans Krauts – and nor must I call Nazis Germans, because it might cause offence.' On the *Fawlty Towers* thing, a spokesman for UKTV explained that 'we regularly make schedule services where necessary to ensure that our channels meet the expectations of our audience'. Had anyone actually complained? Had UKTV asked its audience? Or was it taking fake offence on our behalf? The same attitude is evident outside theatres where trigger warnings disclose what sort of allegedly shocking outrages are in a play: cigarette smoking, fireworks, discriminatory language, scenes of a violent or sexual nature, etc. Trigger warnings are the dribbling get-out clauses of an equivocating arts elite that has weakly accepted the whinges of moral terrorists. Stop telling us what will offend us. This play may contain family dysfunction? Show me a decent play that doesn't.

Third-party grievance has become a way of hammering establishment views into our skulls. Trans people claim to be offended by 'binary' lavatories. Pull the other one – if it's still there. Traditionalists fume about pacifists wearing white poppies. Their indignation is not persuasive. That homo-erotic poem about Jesus that so annoyed Mary Whitehouse: did it really imperil anyone's idea of Christ? Those of us who are moved by the story of Golgotha – Stainer's *Crucifixion* makes my neck-hairs prickle every time I sing it – are not likely to be derailed by something so marginal as a poem in *Gay News*. Religion goes deeper than that. But the people taking offence on my behalf won't know that because they probably don't go to church. Left-wing atheists argue that a hate crime is anything that gives offence, yet they will shrug at blasphemy because they think religion is daft.

Along comes anti-Islamic blasphemy. That makes them gulp a bit. Muslims are an ethnic minority here and when an ethnic minority feels offended, well, racism must be afoot. And yet Islam is so problematic with its attitudes to gay people and women. Dilemmas, dilemmas! They spin in circles. They feel quite dizzy with contradictions. And then, as happens, they all fall down.

Offence-taking is reported at face value. Journalistic scepticism has abdicated. Is it not more likely that many of those anti-Colston protestors in Bristol, and the Oxford students, were having a high old time causing trouble? I don't suppose many people in Britain felt 'insulted' by Cummings going to Co. Durham. They thought he was a hypocrite and they rolled their eyes, yes. But 'offence' was hardly the word. Vandals who spray war memorials with paint are prats. Please don't dignify their petty criminality by claiming it has caused us distress. Instead of being upset, we are more usually unimpressed, some way short of gruntled. But if you wrote *MIFFED* in a *Mail Online* headline, it might not have quite the pinch of *FURY*.

Foreign News

Abroad, the spirit of Oliver Cromwell endures. Singapore does not permit its citizens to chew gum. Indonesia, Pakistan and Saudi Arabia take a dim view of St Valentine's Day. Portugal has strict rules about babies' names, the authorities arguing that parents have a responsibility not a right when it comes to choosing children's names. Diminutives are not allowed. Names must be gender-specific – not for them any of this foolishness of calling girls Brian – and the names must not invite abuse. Mr and Mrs Thomas would not be allowed to call their son Jonathan were they Portuguese and Sir Bob Geldof would have been in trouble. In Iran they are not keen on men with ponytails or long hair, regarding them as effeminate, agents of Western decadence and of being generally unreliable. The mullahs should meet Tosh McDonald, a stalwart of the ASLEF train drivers' union, who was for many years a star turn at the TUC and Labour Party conferences. A burly lad with tattoos on his knuckles and big rings, Tosh would lope up to the lectern, shake his shoulder-length, custardy mane, and proceed to bawl abuse at the capitalist system for the next three minutes until the little red light came on and the presiding officer

Keep your hair on: Tosh and mullah

had the unenviable task of trying to persuade Brother Tosh to leave the stage. By now the conference hall would be in uproar with a rolling boil of applause sweeping the delegates as Tosh denounced Thatcherism and big money and all the various other deficiencies of modern Britain. You can imagine him going down a storm in Tehran at a conference of the Society of Devotees of the Islamic Revolution, but of course he might not make it past the immigration clerks at the airport, or at least not unless he shaved his Princess Rapunzel locks. Rules is rules, *sayidi*.

Iran has also banned mullets (the hairdo, not the fish). Talking of fish, in Rome it is illegal to keep a goldfish in a glass bowl. Why? Water in a bowl is likely to have bad oxygen flow and this can make goldfish blind. How ridiculous. When did you last see a goldfish wearing glasses?

As you approach the staircases at Swindon railway station you are told: 'When on the stairs, please use the handrail.' To make it doubly annoying, the message on Platform 1 places strange emphasis on the 'on'. When *on* the stairs, please use the handrail. Makes me want to scream every time. I had just come *off* the stairs and was heading through the ticket barrier when a policeman, aged *c.*25, told me off for not wearing a mask. He wasn't wearing one either. 'Not necessary this side of the barrier,' he explained. I said it was a damn silly rule. 'Couldn't agree more,' he replied.

Mask Nazis

Police practise some community outreach

Masks were once the preserve of sorcerers and bandits. Primitive witch doctors, when leaping from foot to foot at ceremonial sacrifices, would wear a mask so that onlookers would think 'Crumbs, the spirit is among us' rather than, 'I must say Clive doesn't quite seem himself today.' English highwaymen wore eye masks in part to hide their identity, in part to create an air of menace. Modern bank robbers wear balaclavas for much the same purpose. A human form without a face becomes sinister. The mouth is a vital indicator of someone's mood. The relationship of eyes to the mouth and nose helps us become attracted to potential mates.

Masks make it impossible to 'read' someone. They dehumanise us. They make it harder to be social creatures.

Masks were worn in early theatre to signify tragedy or comedy, or a certain type of character. Venetian carnival masks bestow a dashing anonymity. Death masks remove the life from a face. Though a death mask records accurately the dead person's facial contours, the ensuing image can often be hard to recognise. When people wear masks they cease to be people and they somehow become piggish, like porkers in Orwell's *Animal Farm*. There is something communist about the way masks turn us from individuals into owned beasts, following the rules of superiors who have made mask-wearing mandatory. Masks say: 'We are obedient'.

Is it irrational to feel this way? Maybe. Yet instinct nests far inside us and I, for one, hate masks with a loathing stronger than I can explain. They are uncomfortable and they make my glasses steam and they stink and their straps hurt and they are yet another thing to remember when you leave the house and they make one feel like a Japanese *salariman*. All that is true. But there is also the feeling of entrapment. It is more than the slight obstruction to clean breath. There is a sense of enslavement, somehow of shame, of having been branded, lassoed by cowboys, overcome by oppressors. Rodeo ponies can sense when their freedom is being threatened and they kick. I don't blame them. When told to wear a mask, that is how I feel. Boris Johnson argued that masks had to be worn because we were all potential 'vectors of the virus'. It was the moment I gave up on him. We have always been vectors of all sorts of diseases yet we have not let that browbeat us. Masks were imposed at a time when the economy was in urgent need of revival and virus risk was low. When Boris told me I was a potential vector of disease, I wanted to yell at him that we were also all vectors of economic ill-health. Masks accentuated a sense of abnormality in the country. They frightened people into staying away from town centres.

Yes, fear again. Masks were brought in as a psychological device, allegedly to reassure the Covid neurotics but more to create a mood of public obedience. The motivation was, to borrow a James Thurber line, 'crumplehope and dampenglee'. If you bridled against masks, you were clocked as a troublemaker. Some members of the public took it upon themselves to boss their fellow citizens to 'wear the goddam mask'. This became an intensely party-political thing in the United States, where Donald Trump was a mask sceptic and Joe Biden was pro-masks. In Britain we had no presidential election but in the Twittersphere fanatics depicted non-maskers as would-be murderers. Masks were going to stop the pandemic. They were going to prevent a second wave. They didn't. All they did was deepen public panic and, with mask sceptics staying away from shops, worsen the economic damage. In March 2020 one of the deputy chief medical officers, Jenny Harries, said masks could make the pandemic worse because people would touch them all the time. Jake Dunning, head of emerging infections at Public Health England, said there was 'very little evidence of a widespread benefit' from masks. And when that Danish study came along saying masks were useless, almost no one reported it apart from the *Spectator*, earning a blackout from Facebook. Was this really about health? Or was it about authority imposing itself, an official class determined to make the citizenry listen to its pronouncements with greater reverence in future?

Seinfeld's Soup Nazi: Aryan stock?

Hades erupted in July 2020 when the *Sunday Times*'s Camilla Long wrote a column saying it was a bore to have to wear masks in manicure parlours. Camilla's column carried the headline 'Lighten up, face-mask Nazis.' *Mamma mia*, a hoopla ensued. Social media feeds practically caught fire, such was the level of damnation along the lines of 'Mask Nazis? You can't call us that! We're good people! We're trying to *save* lives. We are Albert Schweitzers, not Albert Speers.' Camilla was accused of equating masks with the Holocaust. How could she be so cruelly disproportionate? Was the genocidal murder of Jews and gypsies and gays not worse than the inconvenience of having to wear a mask? Well, yes. We probably do not need to consult the third umpire for that one. But she had made none of the moral equivalences alleged. The headline used 'Nazi' in an exaggerated, comical way to get across the idea that the fusspots who force others to wear masks can be proper little Hitlers. Oops! Now I've gone and done it myself.

Actually, the day before Camilla's column I used 'mask Nazi' in a *Times* sketch – and nobody complained. Just shows no one reads my stuff. But 'mask Nazi' was not in the headline. The hot-to-trot outrage brigade don't often look beyond the headlines.

It's a wonder that the New York comedian Jerry Seinfeld ever got away with his character the Soup Nazi, a bad-tempered chef. The Soup Nazi's customers would put up with being bullied by him because his soup was so good. Perhaps it was made with Aryan stock. But a 'Soup Nazi'? Gasp. Seinfeld the anti-Semite!!!! Given that he comes from a Jewish family, that seems unlikely. More probably Seinfeld was just teasing petty authoritarianism and the sort of batey foot-stampers who want to micromanage other people.

Anyway, I can't abide masks. Worse, I can't abide the authoritarians who force me to wear one. Nor can I take seriously people who wear one with great self-importance, peacocking their virtue long after the official masks mandate ended. Labour MPs Ben Bradshaw and Matt Western started making a palaver about wearing them in the House of Commons, ripping them off melodramatically when their turn to speak arrived. A form of mask apartheid developed, where everyone on the Labour benches wore one and almost no one on the Tory side bothered. Nicola Sturgeon marched about in a tartan mask. Boris Johnson in a mask looked like a shire horse wearing its lunchtime nosebag. In the Commons cloisters one day I came across the thoroughly decent Ming Campbell, sometime leader of the Lib Dems. A day or so earlier, notices had gone up urging us all to wear masks on the parliamentary estate. It was not a law so I felt able to ignore it. Ming, being a team player, felt he should go along with mask-wearing, even though it steamed up his spectacles. 'I need windscreen wipers,' he wailed, after nearly bumping into me. The mask's straps had bent his ears over themselves. There he was, a grandfatherly, slightly fragile gent of the old school, doing what he felt was his duty – all for possibly no effect whatsoever. It was not just the bossiness of the masks edict I hated. It was the way it took advantage of obedient citizens' decency.

One last thought on masks: how often did we see the Queen wearing one?

Historians claim that the English Civil War of the mid-seventeenth century was fuelled by rows over parliamentary sovereignty, kingly excess and liturgical taste. Maybe. But there was another gulf between the two sides: the Royalist Cavaliers wore soft hats and individual outfits while Cromwell's Roundheads wore helmets and armour. The Cavaliers were careless of personal safety, preferring to stride around in the manner of freeborn Britons, while their Puritan enemies were into the personal protective equipment of the day. They proclaimed a stern belief in the Almighty but they did not want to leave anything to chance. In Covid-hit Britain, Cromwellians would have been mask Nazis.

Care for Clappers

Man days from near-death gives nurses the clap

Emotive coercion moved up a gear at 8 p.m. on Thursday 27 March, 2020. It is rare to be able to date a political phenomenon so precisely, but that was the moment the nation felt moved to stand on doorsteps and clap the NHS. It was replicated the following Thursday, and the Thursday after that. Ten Thursdays in all. At the start it had felt spontaneous. By the end it had become divisive and politicised. Did you do your bit? Did you take part?

One should jolly well hope you did. There'll be trouble otherwise.

When the clapping started, lockdown was a novelty. Pandemical panic was at that point all-engrossing, still quite interesting. We had yet to acquire herd immunity to the socio-political engineering that was taking place. When ninnies drew their lips into goaty bows and bleated 'keep well' or 'stay safe', one had not quite reached the stage of wanting to slap them. Give nurses a clap? Okay. It would be good to have something to do at 8 p.m. – lockdown was so boring – and see if the neighbours had given each other black eyes from being cooped up together so long. Millions of Britons duly stood in their doorways and clapped or hit saucepans or blew bagpipes or did whatever else they fancied in order to signal gratitude for medical professionals. It was not as tuneful as the Italians, who sang arias from their apartment balconies, but it was somehow rather uplifting. The children enjoyed it, too. Yes, all right, Jemima, it's half past eight and we can stop clapping now.

The idea for a British clapalong had come from a Dutch ex-pat, Annemarie Plas, who had heard of similar things in other countries. Ms Plas, a yoga teacher with positive vibes and an engaging smile, stuck the thought on her social media feeds. It was picked up by others, including the Beckhams and the Sussexes. Hard to tell those two couples apart sometimes, isn't it? Victoria Beckham gave the idea a flurry of kisses. See? I'm not such an ice queen. Harry and Meghan, who roll in charitable sentiment rather as terriers will roll in badger crap, said on Instagram that 'during these unprecedented times they need to know we are grateful'. This was in the very same week that the Sussexes, world-leading eco-campaigners that they are, flew from Canada to Los Angeles by private jet. And yet a corner of their big, big hearts was still pumping for the NHS. Yes it was.

With each week the clapping continued, egged on now by the full promotional might of NHS press offices. With each week this national gesture lost a little more of its innocence. Politicians and must do merchants muscled in. They always wreck things. On the second Thursday, a Covid-stricken Boris Johnson was dragged from his sickbed at the top of 10 Downing Street and forced by the broadcasters to clap in the doorway of his official residence, even though he looked waxy with illness and plainly needed to be in bed. A few days later he was admitted to hospital, where he nearly died. Still, he had done his thing. He had clapped. He had denied his political enemies the chance to say, 'See? Boris really *doesn't* care about the health service.'

Jeremy Corbyn loved clapping for the NHS. He hit a makeshift drum and jumped up and down in the street with childish excitement. Socialism was coming home! Rishi Sunak made his observance like a cricket spectator giving sympathetic applause to a losing side. Nicola Sturgeon, wrapped so tightly in imperial purple that she could have been wearing Clingfilm, conjoined two cold palms and grimaced. Around her the temperature dropped at least five degrees. She's the opposite of the kid in the Ready Brek adverts. The Royal Family was pressed into front-line action, the Cambridges' three pretty children clapping for a Twitter message. Match that, Meghan. Sir Keir Starmer QC vouchsafed a photo opportunity to Sky News. The minute's applause had already started when Sir Keir emerged from his north London house accompanied by Lady Starmer. He gave a smile – did he think the applause was for him? – and then hesitantly joined the clapping. A few seconds later he turned to the Sky camera lens and said, 'Have you got what you need?'

Celebrities took clap-clap footage of themselves, to show they cared. Ben Fogle, TV presenter, released a video of his family applauding hard. Competitive clapping. Quick, get it up on social media before anyone else! 'Our heroes,' added goodie-goodie Fogle in a Tweet. John Boyega, an actor, Greg James, a radio presenter, Michelle Collins, a soap star, Posh Spice and her intellectual help-meet in a working man's flat cap: they were all at it, the Beckhams now positively haloed by their early association with the cause. We might be multi-millionaires but we are part of the community. Was Whitehall's honours committee taking note? Give Becks a knighthood! Hospital doctors clapped themselves. Firemen clapped, reminding us that they, too, mattered, and don't forget that when the public sector is next up for a pay rise. The Cardiff Millennium Centre put up the message *Diolch Yn Fawr* NHS, thus ticking two *blychau* in one: sucking up to the NHS and fulfilling their bilingual obligations. At least ten people in Cardiff will have understood what it meant. Bridges were lit, stadia adorned, clock towers had images projected on to them, and photographers were on hand to catch all this and to persuade us – tell us – that our country was one big Richard Curtis film-set, aglow with solidarity under the banner of Saint Aneurin's health service and a rash of ruddy rainbow signs.

And if we opted out? The *Coventry Telegraph* reported the case of a young mother who missed one Thursday's clap because she had fallen asleep. 'A post went on our community Facebook group actually naming and shaming me,' said the woman. 'I was mortified. The post said everyone else turned out and I showed the street up and if I can't spend a minute showing my appreciation I don't deserve to use the NHS if I or my family get ill. I ignored it at the time but I can't get it out of my head, it's really upset me.' There was aggro in the other direction, too. In Winchester, a cross anti-clapper, Teresa Skelton, whipped out a megaphone and started bawling at neighbours for 'clapping like seals' and for their gullibility in falling for Boris Johnson's conspiracy to wreck the British economy. Ms Skelton's pro-clap neighbours responded – naturally – with another sustained and even louder volley of applause, trying to drown out her words. Feel the community love, guys.

Voices from the care sector complained that it should be 'clap for carers' because 'clap the NHS' did not include nurses in old people's homes. That god-almighty-irritant Matt Hancock, the health secretary, soon produced a special lapel badge to replace his usual NHS badge.

The new one said 'CARE' and would, claimed Mr Hancock, be pinned to the lapels of the nation's 1.5 million care workers and help them to secure advantages such as being allowed to jump to the front of supermarket queues and securing discounts at certain shops. Three months later Lord Rogan (Ulster Unionist Party) submit-

Hancock and his CARE pin: watch out for the little prick

ted a parliamentary question: 'To ask HM Government how many CARE badges have been distributed to social care workers.' Back came the answer that just 15,000 badges had been distributed. But others were going to be dished out 'in due course', just you see.

The Left, which one might have expected to revel in this dewy-eyed twaddle, started to become huffy that Conservative ministers were in on the act. Cheering the socialist health service is all very well when Labour politicians and trade unionists do it, but when Tories take part it becomes cynical and despicable. The *Guardian* reported that doctors felt the clapping was a 'sentimental' practice – clinicians do not approve of sentimentality – and 'clapping distracts from the real issues'. Dr Sophie Behrman, an NHS psychiatrist, said: 'As an NHS psychiatrist, I am aware of medical colleagues feeling guilty for not being able to do enough. No one feels like a hero.'

Back in London, yoga teacher Annemarie Plas unlocked her ankles from the lotus position and realised that her sweet idea had been warped and hashtagged and blood-suckered and turned into an instrument of control and self-promotion. A YouGov poll found that a third of Britons felt that the Thursday-night clap had become politicised. Ms Plas said it was time to stop the clapping. For a while, at least. And yet a National Clap for Our Carers Day has now been announced for 2021 and Clap for Our Carers has been turned into a not-for-profit movement complete with T-shirts and sponsors and press officers and web designers. At the bottom of the official website is a legal disclaimer denouncing profiteering. 'The Clap for Carers logo and brand assets,' it says, 'can be used freely without restriction so long as they are not used in a manner which could be considered as negative, detrimental or damaging to the essence and vision of the movement, or its founder Annemarie Plas.' Too late, dear. Too late.

A Patient Writes . . .

Is the NHS worth clapping? General practitioners, on an average of £110,000 a year, hardly broke a sweat during the pandemic. Many conducted consultations by telephone. Working from home is all right for insurance company employees but is it not important for a doctor to be able to prod your lumps and bumps? Stethoscopes do not work down a telephone line.

Dentists were even idler. I went down with toothache at the start of Lockdown 1. Stabbing agony. 'Take some paracetamol,' was all the receptionist at our dental surgery could say. She promised to let me know when the dentist would be back at her chair. Nine months later there has still come no word. For years the dentistry profession lectured us about oral hygiene and regular checks. That clinical mission evaporated. One dreads to think what will happen to mouth cancer rates in future. I gave up on my NHS dentist and went private, paying a fortune. One had images of private healthcare as in the adverts: smiling receptionists, vases of flowers, a service attentive to the patient's every whim. Not quite. 'Please' and 'Thank you' went unuttered. Before paying, you had to stand behind a yellow line on the floor. It was like immigration at New York's JFK airport, without the charm.

At around the same time, my brother Alexander became seriously ill. He was told that unless he had an operation within days, he would die. The local hospital said, 'No, you can't have an operation that quickly because you need to go through a two-week check for coronavirus.' He pointed out that in two weeks he would be a goner. The NHS was unimpressed. Happily, his local MP took up his cause and he was admitted to hospital. He wrote this account of his stay:

> *Lying on my hospital bed after yet another stupidly disturbed night, it is easy to resort to polemic. In truth, there is as much to applaud as to despair for. The skill and confidence of the surgeons and their teams, despite the ancient environment (the facilities are more Florence Nightingale than Chicago Hope). The improved quality of food. The empathy, care and effort of (many of) the nurses doing stomach-churning work. And at point of delivery, it is free.*
>
> *But. So much is wrong that could easily be set right. Some of it comes down to common sense that appears to have gone on permanent furlough. The rest is probably about control by one human over another.*
>
> *My ward is full of men in recovery. That means rest and sleep for drained bodies. Day and night merge as anaesthetics and healing demand their ransoms. So, why is the ward blaring mindless zoo-radio shows all day? A comatose patient has his TV on loudly. The wards can provide expensive TVs but not cheap headsets?*
>
> *Why do the ward's 1980s strip lights need to be ruthlessly switched on at 7 a.m. sharp and stay on till 11 p.m.? Every bed has its own electric light, after all. Nurses have the*

night-lighting they require to guide them. For helpless patients it is impossible to escape this unrelenting light torture. How is this not about control?

Why do two nurses, who have the unenviable night shift, spend all night gossiping and talking at the top of their voices? This stuff is not about training. It is about thoughtfulness. Some shifts whisper. Others seem to make a point of letting you know that they are 'working' (loudly) for you. A brief memo will suffice. I am happy to write it: 'Shut the fuck up' should do it.

Most urgently, when the desperate patient presses his call bell, or when the morphine drip bag is empty and the beep-beeeep-beeeeep alarms go off, that sound is of such a pitch and repetitive intensity that it can be easily heard in the next shire. Not just by the nurses but by the other patients. Nurses ignoring it for ten minutes is a mind-control deviance that might interest the War Crimes panel at The Hague.

And why, when beds are so scarce, do certain teams not work weekends? It has meant my cost of occupancy being extended for Saturday and Sunday nights, so a box-checker can kiss me goodbye on Monday. I could have been packed off on Friday. Control again.

So, whilst there is so much to praise with the NHS, there is a list of things which any good manager could sort out in a day. That it doesn't get done suggests there is a sense of showing who is in control (clue: it's not you); it's a power-play where people get dealt their humiliation.

He had a point, hadn't he?

Visit to the Engine Room

The time has come to visit the gubbins of the bossy mind. You report at its entrance and are confronted by shiny gates. A side door swings open. You are guided to a vestibule where you are checked for hygiene, citizen number and intent. Security is paramount. One can never be too careful. Announcements remind you to wear a face covering at all times. There is a temperature check and, built into the floor, industrial scales to make sure you are not irresponsibly fat. A *sprrrrrt* of spray checks that you have not recently handled any saltpetre, sheep faeces or copies of the *Spectator*. 'Thank you, citizen, and welcome,' says a unisex voice. The bossy mind cannot be faulted for courtesy. If it is asperity you seek, visit the other side of the street where the freedom lovers live. Bossocrats are neat. They are law-abiding. Good people. Your footsteps echo on the griddled floor, down rigid corridors whose beams are stamped with the words *sdelano v Islington*. There are no windows. A machine room is reached. Cogs and wheels gleam. Staircases of galvanised steel spiral upwards until the eye can see no more. There is perhaps the faintest smell of spearmint toothpaste. In the standard of its fittings, the precision of the joins, rivets, nickel-plated eyelets, chains and tacks and grommets and snaps, all is orderly. There are no squashy chairs. Bunk-bed mattresses fold away into hidden compartments, grudging acknowledgement of the biological function of sleep. Vitamin capsules incorporate dietary preferences within the envelope of approved cultural variations. When did you last see garlic or cream in a science-fiction space film? There is no wine list. Chlorinated water – carcinogenic yet 'vital for your teeth' – spurts from plastic nozzles and has been filtered to international best practice. All else is devoted to progress, meetings, targets, reports. You are told that you may, if you really wish, view the inspection log and certificates of approval from the supervising ministry. But if you do ask to see them, you will be put down as a troublemaker.

Welcome!

Something is missing. You cannot put your finger on it but there is an incompleteness. This mind meets most of the usual requirements such as taste and numeracy, hearing and reason. It can process language. Looking around the chambers, you are impressed by the cleanliness. There is an efficiency here. No clutter. Nor even any waste-paper bins or chutes to take away the rubbish. And that is when you realise: there are no ducts. A normal mind has channels to maintain flows of that essential fluid, scepticism. Scepticism breaks down logic, just as bile breaks down fat. In the bossy mind, logic accumulates until it reaches overload.

Your curiosity has been noted and you are told to leave. Social-distance arrows on the floor lead you to the exit pod. After returning your 'VISITOR' badge, you are deposited outside, where you began. And inside the mind, an automatic deep-cleansing cycle has begun, to expunge all risk of contamination.

Philosophers are clever, are they not? They exist (if they *do* exist) to work out the meaning of life. They devise 'laws' and identify systems and they tell us how to achieve happiness. And yet: many of them are round the twist and very few are cheerful. Friedrich Nietzsche pushed himself forward as an expert on God and Übermenschlichkeit but you would not have wanted to leave him alone in your house with a box of matches. That moustache gave things away. Friedrich was a fruit-cake. Socrates thought he knew best. Gosh, he liked to lay down the law. Yet his most frequent question to others was 'Are you sure about that?' He was plainly a right

Nietzsche: spaghetti Bolognese not easy with that moustache

'oooh, I wouldn't do it like that if *I* were you'. He quibbled and quibbled and quibbled and quibbled until they made him drink hemlock. Not such a bright spark, after all. Jean-Paul Sartre spouted the theory of existentialism, which in short holds that we are makers of our own fortune and should crack on with life. On this he was most insistent. He scorned others for being irrational. Yet show him a lobster or a shrimp or a crab, and he whimpered like a baby. Such was his terror of crustaceans that he once had a panic attack on the Côte d'Azur when his popsy, Simone de Beauvoir, tried to lure him into the sea.

Mind you, the sight of de Beauvoir in a swimming costume, ever-present fag sticking out of her mouth, must have been pretty terrifying. She was another who loved to lay down the law, words gushing out of her, self-doubt entirely absent. Princess Anne minus the gumboots. Last, there was Hannah Arendt, noble critic of totalitarianism. She disliked being told what to do, and good for her. But if you watch footage of her being interviewed, there is one thing (apart from her voice, which was almost as deep as Henry Kissinger's): when she talked she kept pointing her finger at her interlocutor and shaking it like a deficient ballpoint pen. Arendt, critic of dictators, was herself, literally, *eine Finger-Wagger.*

Scots Do Porridge

Mr Mackay and First Minister

Campaigners for an independent Scotland once demanded 'a free nation'. Just you wait till the English have gone, then we'll be liberated and be able to do as we wish: that was the battle cry. It stirred my juices, and I'm not even Scottish. But when coronavirus came along, 'freedom' was parked round the back of Bute House and stuck on bricks. Nicola Sturgeon, the Nats' stiletto-stamping guv'nor, saw there was more political potency – power for her personally – in Scotland being kept at home, doing what she and her stooges ordered. Scots were thus admonished and incarcerated and even denied strong drink by the peppery wee shriveller. Sturgeon had turned into Mr Mackay, head prison warder from TV's *Porridge*.

They had a miserable time. The Scottish National Party, however, was in clover. Opinion polls suggested that support for independence was rising almost as fast as Covid cases. Even when infection rates were lower than England's, yet England's people were allowed out more, the Edinburgh authorities kept their boots to people's necks. Scots looked south and may well have felt envy. Never mind. They felt different. That was what the separatists wanted. Ties of British solidarity were fraying.

La Sturgeon had stumbled across this book's core theme: interference and oppression and executive high-handedness – in short, bossiness – is how you establish a name for yourself. Leaving citizens to mind their own business is a non-starter for the ambitious politico. History books show us this. They are full of conquerors and revolutionaries and little corporals. There are not many pages reserved for rulers who gazed out of their palace windows and said, 'Tell you what, let's leave the masses alone today.' We read about Ivan the Terrible, not Ivan the Inactive. She was Bloody – not Laidback – Mary. Only in television comedy do you find a sergeant like Arthur Wilson or Ernest G. Bilko. Leaders seize power. That's what they do. If they distribute choices as if scattering Trill to budgies, they may well leave their kingdoms more prosperous but they will not be memorialised. Calls for deregulation or bonfires of the quangos or reductions in the numbers of MPs are doomed to failure because the thing that drives politics is patronage – the power to give underlings jobs that will allow them to boss people about. Patronage usually only changes hands. On the rare occasions that it evaporates, that is because there has been a change in science – i.e., the invention of the contraceptive pill, which altered the male–female power balance, or geography, such as the silting up of New Romney, originally one of the mighty Cinque Ports but now stranded a mile from the Kent coast. You can still see a mooring ring in the church wall at New Romney. Tugs once tethered there. Now residents use it to park their pugs.

For Mrs Mackay and her Scots Nats, the tide was racing. Covid was putting them centre-stage. Every death was an opportunity. Downing Street tried to make the big decisions but Ms Sturgeon soon barged them off the ball. That could not be done by making the Scottish lockdown lighter. Severity! That was the route to glory. When Downing Street held daily televised press conferences in the afternoon, she held hers at lunchtime. That created an impression that she was leading the fight. And she made sure she herself was on parade every day. There was none of that silly idea Boris Johnson had of allowing colleagues to share the limelight. Nor did she umm and arhh like Boris, or try to crack jokes. She was strict and shook her head. She always made sure her decisions were tougher, even if it harmed Scottish business. If England went two steps, she went three. When Boris chose a three-tier system, she found five. Harsher, snarlier, tighter, tauter: the politics of this were cynical. Scottish students were made to feel like prisoners – with Sturgeon jangling her keys – but the cause of independence was being boosted. We're going to be as bossy as you but we're going to be bossy in our own, wee, meanminded way.

Mark Drakeford watched this and thought, 'I wouldn't mind a piece of that action.' At the name 'Mark Drakeford', your grey matter struggles. Drakeford, Drakeford. At which point you go back to sleep, the name subconsciously working as a sedative. He has that effect. Who or what was Mark Drakeford? That rich footballer who kept talking about free food for poor kids? A *Jackanory* presenter from the programme's paedo-jumper phase in the 1980s? A flower-power-era pop singer who took too many antidepressants? No. Mark Drakeford is the first minister of Wales and, before the pandemic, a figure whose name meant nothing to 99 per cent of households, even in Splott. Not one of life's showstoppers. He was once a social studies lecturer at Swansea University, where he acquired Dave Spart views. He disapproved of the Royal Family. He read the *Morning Star*. He wore the sort of crepe-soled shoes that squeak on a wet pavement. Brother Drakeford, a loss to the undertaking business, became a backroom operator in Cardiff politics. When big, hairy Rhodri Morgan was Wales's first minister, Drakeford was the wonk who made sure there were sufficient pencils in the stationery cupboard. When Jeremy Corbyn stood for leader of Labour, drongo Drakeford was about the only apparatchik west of Chepstow who backed him. Corbyn was so amazed that anyone had gone out on a limb for him that the favour was returned when Morgan's successor, Carwyn Jones, quit. Arise, First Minister Drakeford. For more than a year, Drakeford's leadership was near-invisible. He could walk into a room with the Newport County reserve goalkeeper and the goalie would be the one mobbed by autograph hunters.

Like his friend Jeremy, he enjoyed growing vegetables but even at the Pontcanna allotments there were fellow gardeners who found they could look right through him without remembering a thing he had said – or grown. His campaign for the leadership was so low-key that when they had a whip-round at the Cynon Valley Labour Party, it raised just £145 plus a couple of buttons, one Tufty Club badge and a Croatian ten-lipa coin left over from Jones the Miser's last holiday to Dubrovnik. When impressive politicians arrive in office, grafters sidle up to them and try to bribe them with freebies. Mark Drakeford's register of interests showed that he received only one gift: a hamper of cheese. He gave it away, one hopes before the Caws Preseli became too pongy. Decent but dull, Drakeford.

The Welsh Assembly was sliding further into meaninglessness. At the start of the pandemic, Drakeford held a few press conferences but hardly anyone watched and those who did found them so stupendously boring that they had to be restored by defibrillator paddles. Most of this time, Wales enjoyed slightly looser restrictions than the rest of the UK (despite a brief attempt to stop residents driving more than five miles from home, which meant some Welsh farmers couldn't visit their sheep). We went there on holiday – three lovely nights on Anglesey – precisely because you did not have to wear a mask in shops. Until, until, the dullest man in British politics saw what Nicola Sturgeon was up to in Scotland – and decided to go the full Owain Glyndŵr. Suddenly the Welsh government went Covid bonkers. A 'firebreak' plan was announced – they couldn't call it a 'circuit breaker' because that was what the hated English called it – and the principality was whacked by business closures and Welsh landlords responded by banning the First Minister from their premises. Welsh police were instructed to patrol entrance roads from England and stop people entering from plague-infested areas. Most nuttily of all, Drakeford ruled that only 'essential' goods could be sold in supermarkets. Aisles containing 'non-essential goods' such as clothes, cooking pots, baby food and, good grief, sanitary towels, were sealed off from customers. One man was so enraged that he went round a supermarket ripping off the plastic tape that prevented people from entering the banned aisles. And Chris Noden, 38, turned up at the Newport branch of Tesco in nothing but his socks, gym shoes and skimpy underpants – plus mask, naturally. He was stopped by a security guard who told him he could not enter the shop in a state of undress. Mr Noden explained that he wanted to buy clothes. The guard would not relent. Mr Noden's wife said the Welsh government had ruled clothes were 'not essential'. The guard failed to see the funny side. Authority often does.

Every school needs at least one member of staff who is hopeless at keeping order. My friend Anthony, a gentle soul, fancied a career in education and began teacher-training at a secondary school. In the first class a boy called Rivers started passing an imaginary parcel to his neighbour. Anthony proved incapable of stopping this. Rivers and his mates had spotted they could rag their new teacher – and they soon drove Anthony out of teaching. He became a successful businessman and, as it happens, one of life's rebels (if you can't beat 'em,

---

join 'em). If children learn how far they can push authority, it will help them later in life when dealing with their bosses. Rhodes Boyson MP, a former headmaster, observed that 'if the teacher is not in charge of the class, someone else is'. And his name might well be Rivers.

House Training

I give the orders around here

John Bercow's Speakership of the Commons (2009–2019) was a time of autocratic tantrums. A tetchier hobgoblin would be hard for any dramatist to present on stage. Audiences would say 'Come off it, this character is over-done.' But Bercow was no work of fiction. The little boiler was all too real. His time as Speaker was marked by foot-stamping bates, oily favouritism, rampant egomania. It saw Olympic-standard windbaggery and allegations of bias more naked than any bikini twanger on the sand dunes at Cap d'Agde. This red, blistering tomato snarled at his enemies and sneered at the convention that Speakers should be dignified referees. He called MPs 'stupid women' even while presenting himself as a champion of feminism. He snapped and yacked and when he gave his rulings his little pinkies would stick out at an angle, like woodworm sticking their snorkels above decks to savour the breeze.

Bercow degraded the Speakership and he must have known that. Why did he do it? Because it was all about him. The worse he behaved, the more attention he gained, and that made it harder for opponents to topple him. In the arena of the Commons, criticism from opponents bakes you ever tighter into your ramekin dish. John Bercow was a classic example of obnoxiousness as a political survival mechanism. You could almost call it Trumpian, except Trump lost. As, eventually, did Bercow.

His Speakership was powered by negative ions from the start. He was elected to the Chair by Labour MPs who wanted to annoy the Conservatives. By that narrow measure, the Bercow years were a success: he annoyed the hell out of the Tories. Along came coalition. The government had a majority but David Cameron's Conservatives did not. Bercow picked enough fights with them to secure continued support from non-Cameroons. That is how he operated. When it looked as if Theresa May might romp home in 2017, Bercow's people put it about that he would go quietly. The tune changed when May failed to secure a majority. Suddenly Bercow saw another opportunity for himself. He could become the Speaker who helped parliament overturn a referendum.

Greedy for historical recognition, he became even more despotic and started collaborating with Remain ultras. Things became so deranged that Bercow resorted to rewriting the rules. Clever lawyers said he was within his rights. The public just saw a knot of pro-EU parliamentarians trying to overturn a democratic result, and at the front of it all was a finger-stabbing cuss who seemed to be treating the whole country with a scurvy disregard. The 2017–2019 parliament was a time of screaming, taut unpleasantness. If it had had a musical accompaniment, it would have been Bernard Herrmann's violins from *Psycho* with John Bercow as the conductor.

His public persona had long been a construct. The poshed-up accent. The passive-aggressive mateyness. I remember a telephone call in 2002 when he told me what he thought of Iain Duncan Smith's leadership of the Conservatives – not much – and he oozed false compliments, telling me I was 'a very great man'. He didn't mean a word of it. It was the sort of thing Nicholas Soames used to boom, but Soames did it with a twinkle. Bercow did it with a clumsy insincerity. His alleged spiritual shift from hard Right to soapy Left was similarly unconvincing. The runty Monday Club racist (I first saw him causing trouble at a Tory conference fringe event I was reporting in the late 1980s) started presenting himself, from about 1999, as a convert to minority rights. Where once his best pal had been the apartheid apologist John Carlisle, now he was sucking up to Michael Portillo and soon Gordon Brown. God knows what they thought of him. Like many late converts, Bercow overdid it. His ardour for equalities was signalled clunkily. He preached to tell us how worthy he was. He certainly had intellectual gifts, not least a grasp of arcane procedure. He mobilised Erskine May the way crafty accountants will slalom through the tax code. But Speakers are supposed to follow the spirit as well as the small print of the rules.

The public couldn't bear him. Voters were so angry at the way he helped Remainers to delay our departure from the EU that they voted to 'get Brexit done'. In the end, he harmed his allies. He quit the Speakership, pocketed a big pension and was overlooked for a peerage. He was expected to spend 2020 touring the world giving lectures to foreign institutions. Alas, the pandemic got in the way. At the start of Lockdown 1 he posted a peculiar video of himself leading his family in physical jerks. Then came Lockdown 2, and Lockdown 3. Poor Sally. Incarcerated with her strutting bantam thrice in one year. She didn't deserve that.

Final Whistle

Constable, arrest that man for hate crime

Great Grimsby's Melanie Onn was one of the more cheerful Labour MPs. She had some pep about her, striding in to the Commons and plonking herself down near the likes of Stephen Pound and Kevin Brennan at the top of the gangway on the opposition benches. It was a noisy part of the chamber known for its ripe heckles: 'Gerronwivit!', 'Rubbish!', 'Your back wheel's going round!' Anything to put off the minister at the despatch box. Ms Onn would sit there, loving the fun. Outwardly, she was a photogenic change from her predecessor, the shaggy, shambling Austin Mitchell who always looked as if he might have pebbles of mouldering pork pie in his trouser pockets; but, like old Austin, young Melanie had a ready laugh. She threw herself into the hurly-burly of the *chaise parlementaire*. Politically, there was a problem: her constituency was strongly pro-Brexit, whereas she and much of the parliamentary Labour Party were not. In the 2016 referendum she supported Remain. When the country voted for Brexit, she took the proper view that it was time for her to support leaving the EU. That now created trouble for her in Westminster with Labour colleagues who wanted to stop Brexit. How could Onn regain favour with the metropolitan Labour Party? Maybe an eye-catching speech on something political would do the trick.

In March 2018 she was granted a Westminster Hall debate with the title 'Misogyny As a Hate Crime'. Had she only left it at that, there might have been no problem. But Onn wanted to create bow waves. That is how you prosper at Westminster. Few people take notice of Westminster Hall debates unless there is advance hype. Five days before the debate, the political correspondent of the *Grimsby Telegraph*, Patrick Daly, reported that Ms Onn was going to call for wolf-whistling to be classified a hate crime. Daly was one of the lobby's more reliable scribes. His account was perfectly truthful. But was wolf-whistling worthy of Ms Onn's stunt? It may be vulgar, even chauvinistic, but a 'hate crime'? A woman walks down the street and a bloke whistles at her to show that he thinks she's a cracker: was that to be placed on a par with racism and genocide? As an eighteen-year-old I was wearing shorts one summery Gloucestershire day when I was eyed up by an older woman who shouted, 'Phwoarr – look at those legs!' I laughed at her and she hooted back. Melanie Onn wanted that sort of thing, at least if it happened to women, to become an arrestable offence. It would also become a hate crime if men stood 'too close' to women on public transport. 'These things might be considered "banter" or flirtatious,' said Onn, 'but if they are received as unwelcome then it can be tantamount to harassment, even in a one-off case.' This was the 'it's a crime if we think it is' theory. She wanted the rest of the country to follow a pilot scheme in Nottingham in which the police defined misogyny hate crimes as 'incidents against women that are motivated by an attitude of a man towards a woman and includes behaviour targeted towards a woman by men simply because they are a woman'. If you stand up when a woman enters the room, as I was taught to do, you could be in trouble with Nottinghamshire Plod.

Patrick Daly's *Grimsby Telegraph* article certainly created the desired stir. Ms Onn had waggled her shoulders in a political sense and was suddenly the focus of media pala-ver, provoking earnest debate in the *Daily Mirror* and *Guardian* and elsewhere. Suddenly her support for Brexit – on which she had followed the wishes of her constituents – was forgotten by the metropolitan Left and she became a modern Emmeline Pankhurst. Harriet Harman herself expressed support for the idea, and in identity politics that was as good as a blessing from the Holy Mother. Onn's bid to criminalise wolf-whistles did not lead to a change in the law but she had shown her right-on virtues to the comrades. She had given ogling blokes a stern reminder of twenty-first-century gender-power structures. What a stalwart Sister. There was just one problem: the voters of Grimsby were little impressed. They thought she was being ridiculous. A year later, when they went to their polling stations, they booted Melanie Onn out of office and chose a Conservative for the first time since 1945. And now, when poor Melanie walks down the street or corridor, no one pays her any attention. At all.

Sports commentators no longer describe the action. Adamant that sport is a science rather than simply a game, they feel they must interpret the psychology of the players. The rugby was on Channel 4 and the England winger caught a high kick near the Irish corner and scored. 'That,' said the commentator, one of those shouty women with a butch voice, 'is a *massive statement* by Jonny May.' No it wasn't. He had scored a good try. That was all.

The Eyes Have It

Covid gave the police a chance to boss us around as never before. Emergency powers, ooh yes, don't mind if I do. They could pounce on sunbathers in the park, break up barbecues, arrest people for not wearing masks – it was fill-yer-police-boots time. Cops in Derbyshire used drones to spy on fell walkers who should have been staying at home and saving the NHS. Officers told shops to stop selling Easter eggs ('non-essential items, *sir*') and a man in Manchester was pulled over for delivering food to the needy. There were stories of cops taping off park benches to stop joggers stopping for a sit-down when they were taking their one permitted piece of exercise per day. No slouching was permitted. You could either stay at home or keep moving. The chief constable of Northamptonshire, Nick Adderley, decided we needed to hear from him. He intended to start checking people's supermarket trolleys to make sure they were not buying fripperies. A 'hard core' of citizens was flouting the rules and 'if things don't improve, and we don't get the compliance we would expect, then the next stage will be roadblocks and it will be stopping people to ask why they are going, where they are going'. It was the Towcester Taliban.

Given how the police were behaving with Covid, it was just as well Melanie Onn failed to criminalise wolf-whistles. Otherwise it might have been, 'Right, PC Worboys, put on this short skirt and crop-top and walk past that building site in your transvestite high heels. Sergeant Tosser and the boys will be hiding round the corner in one of our riot vans and the moment anyone wolf-whistles you, Tosser and his lads will leap into action and Taser the alleged whistler on suspicion of hate crime.'

The heavy-handed questioning of the late Field Marshal Lord Bramall and the search of his house; dawn raids and the much-hyped arrests of sixty-seven journalists during the phone-tapping scandal; the mistreatment of Cliff Richard and Paul Gambaccini and Jimmy Tarbuck and Matthew Kelly: there were signs, long before Covid, that the police were going a bit mad. On 21 July 2005, Islamist extremists attacked London's public transport system for the second time that month. The capital was in a state of anxiety. Such was the police's eagerness to grab someone's collar that, the next day, officers trailed an innocent electrician, Jean Charles de Menezes, as he made his way to work. He was Brazilian and police decided he was a wrong 'un because he had 'Mongolian eyes'. As Mr de Menezes made his way to Stockwell Tube station, one of his tails failed to get a proper look at him because the copper was having a slash. Gold command was consulted. Gold command said 'code red', which meant stop the suspect from travelling on the Tube. By now Mr de Menezes was blamelessly sitting in a Tube train, waiting for it to head north. The police entered the carriage, grabbed him and shot him not once but, just to be sure, eleven times, seven of those in the head. By the time they were finished, the body of 27-year-old Mr de Menezes was unrecognisable.

The 'gold command' officer in charge of this operation was Cressida Dick. Twelve years later she was made commissioner of the Metropolitan police and was much fêted by establishment commentators. The *Guardian* might normally have questioned the promotion of an officer with a cock-up as bad as the de Menezes killing on her record, but Cressida Dick was lauded. She was gay. She had done the Matrix course of Common Purpose, a charity which offers politically correct leadership development to rising elites. Dick was 'one of us', as the *Guardian* might never phrase it. Jean Charles de Menezes's family in Brazil was horrified by her promotion to commissioner – 'the message is that police officers can act with impunity' – but that was trumped by Dick's value as a detective and, one sensed, by her bossocracy brownie points.

Today's police seldom investigate minor thefts. Vandalism of monuments (unless it becomes big news) goes unpunished. Drug-taking in the street? Fine by us, say the police. They'll dance at the Notting Hill Carnival, even while the stink of skunk cannabis nearby makes your head swim. But they do love a hate crime – and it could soon get worse. The Law Commission proposes that people should be prosecuted for what they say in their homes. Until now there has been a privacy exemption guaranteeing free speech in homes, but the busybodies of the commission feel that exemption should be removed because it is 'inconsistent'. Of course, removing the exemption might also create more work for lawyers. Members of the Law Commission include two journalists, Joshua Rozenberg and Bronwen Maddox. What the hell are they doing getting mixed up with anything that could see citizens arrested for what they say in privacy at home? And don't think you could get out of trouble by claiming that something you said was a joke. Paul Chambers tried that. He was the young Yorkshireman who, during snow in 2010, posted a joke on Twitter about how he'd feel like 'blowing up' his local airport if it did not reopen for him to fly to see his girlfriend. The police decided this was 'menacing' and Chambers was found guilty on a Communications Act transgression and fined. He lost his job. Three appeals later, and only after Chambers was supported by the likes of Stephen Fry and Al Murray, was the conviction quashed. As one of his lawyers argued, John Betjeman was lucky to get away with, 'Come, friendly bombs, and fall on Slough.'

'Bomber' Betjeman

If you spring your nonagenarian mother from the old people's home where she is miserable, as 73-year-old Ylenia Angeli did in Humberside in November 2020, you may be arrested. If you fail to wear a mask on a train like father-of-five Anthony Baldwin, you will have pepper spray squirted in your face by a member of the Merseyside constabulary. Baldwin had offended other members of the public by sneezing. Was pepper spray really the best thing? Aaaaaaa-chooooo. Consistency is not a police strong point. Steve Bray, an unpleasant man who screamed 'Stop Brexit' outside Parliament for three years after the EU referendum, went untouched by the police. But when a 72-year-old woman meekly protested against the loss of liberties during Lockdown 2, she was brutally carted away by four officers.

The historian David Starkey, a provocative right-winger, was always going to be a target for today's politicised police. For years he pricked the Left on Radio 4's *Moral Maze*. He had done so with a catty turn of phrase. I met him once at a Hungarian Embassy event. He was formidably well read but he talked rather a lot, particularly after a few glasses of Tokaji. In June 2020, Starkey gave a YouTube interview to a young Brexiteer, Darren Grimes. In the course of remarks about the Black Lives Matter protests, Starkey said: 'Slavery was not genocide otherwise there wouldn't be so many damn blacks in Africa or in Britain, would there?' A more experienced interviewer would have jumped on this to say, 'Hang on, Starkey, you can't call them "damn blacks",' but Grimes failed to do so. The comment went unnoticed until it was aired and then the roof fell in on David Starkey. The

Metropolitan Police, by now under the command of Dame Cressida Dick, pulled in both Starkey and Grimes on suspicion of inciting racial hatred. The police let them sweat for a month before dropping the matter but it was still logged as a 'non-crime' hate incident. Why? It was either a crime or it was not, and if not, there should be no reason to record it. Or do the police simply yield to political pressure from lobbying groups? We're back to the moral terrorists, letting it be known that unless the authorities yield to certain demands there will be a public stink. Now came a backlash, with free-speech supporters infuriated that Starkey and Grimes had been strung up on the gibbet for thought crime. Which caused more racial disharmony, here: the original YouTube interview, which hardly anyone would have watched, or the ensuing hoo-hah and police overreaction? You might have expected Dame Cressida, of all people, to accept that people sometimes make disastrous misjudgements. After all, it could have been worse. Starkey could have made a comment about people having 'Mongolian eyes'.

Gong Fishing

One way the bossocracy imposes control is by giving itself prizes. Its sets itself up as the arbiter of public esteem. But its medals, doctorates, fellowships, awards – gongs – are little to do with what the public thinks. They are more an implement of group self-assertion and mutual encouragement. Join the elite and be decorated. Equally, if you displease the clique you will be stripped of your commendations and expelled from the magic circle. Prizes create leverage.

After David Starkey stepped on that landmine by saying 'damned blacks', retribution came swiftly. In addition to being shredded by publishers, he was relieved of numerous honours: his Medlicott Medal from twenty years earlier was 'withdrawn'; Lancaster University revoked his honorary degree, Cambridge's Fitzwilliam College washed its hands of him, some crappy university south of London 'launched a formal review of his honorary graduate status', the Mary Rose Trust 'accepted his resignation' as a trustee, the Royal Historical Society decided he was history and cancelled his fellowship and the Society of Antiquaries of London decided he was no longer so collectible. Life would have been less bruising for Starkey had he never accepted those 'damned' honours in the first place. Vanity, vanity. But why had those organisations decorated him in the first place? Was it for his intellectual muscle? That was surely unaltered by his sinful comment. Or had they decorated him because he had been on telly and was famous and might give them some stardust? Oh. That doesn't seem quite so estimable of them after all, does it? Yet this is how honours work: more symbiotic than you think.

It is all a bit of a con. The public thinks these things are judged on raw merit. Insiders know it is more about sending a message, and politics. And so we end up with knighthoods for dozy and corrupt parliamentary backbenchers. We have OBEs awarded on a quota basis to people because they come from certain communities rather than because they are genuinely brilliant. Annual accolades such as the Booker Prize and the Turner Prize have been devalued. Few people in journalism believe that the various categories of the Orwell Prize are judged on merit. George Orwell would have laughed at how calculating it has all become. At the BBC Sports Personality of the Year you can almost hear the agendas grinding. The Nobel Peace Prize, named after the man who invented dynamite, has not been the same since it went to that enthusiastic dropper of napalm, Henry Kissinger. They gave it to Barack Obama in the first year of his presidency. Pure sucking-up. And then it was given to a source of unending sweetness and light, the European sodding Union. This clunkiness is even more prevalent with minor awards. Take the BBC Woman's Hour Power List, an attempt to list the most influential women in the country. In 2020 it was decided to make the list eco-focused. The top person? Caroline Lucas, the only Green MP at Westminster. Was she really more influential on eco-policy than the six women who sat in the cabinet? Yet none of them even made the list, whereas those who did included: a fifteen-year-old climate activist, the co-founder of Extinction Rebellion, the Future Generations Commis-sioner for Wales, an environmental correspondent of the *Guardian* and someone from the Peak District Mosaic Club. The BBC happily puts its name to this manipulative twaddle.

Few understand the gongs game better than Dame Alan Rusbridger, the Harry Potter-lookalike former *Guardian* editor who now reposes at the Principal's Lodgings, Lady Margaret Hall, Oxford, OX2 6QA, aka Duneditin. Having driven the *Guardian* towards financial peril, Alan retreated to Oxford in 2015. Aged 67, he must now rub along on rather less than the £455,000 a year he accepted when running the anti-plutocratic *Guardian*. And yet, becoming an Oxford master was an agreeable parachute. Lady Margaret Hall's accounts for 2019 record that one of the trustees is recorded to be on an annual whack of £107,999. It may be fair to surmise this is the college's tousle-haired principal. Add to that a spacious residence (with a housekeeper on £10 an hour for twenty hours a week to do his dusting and ironing and to make his bed), dining rights, the command of a secretary and a head of communications, good rail connections to London, plus the status and patronage that a middle-ranking Oxbridge college bestows. Our

Latin-spouting Old Cranleighan class warrior has done all right for himself. Pension entitlements, an Oxford cellar, gracious halls, the opportunity to play Pied Piper to rising generations, and he still gets to be fêted as a tribune of egalitarianism. It is convenient that the head of college at LMH is called Principal and not Master. Alan would not have liked being called Master. It would have been a bit *Uncle Tom's Cabin*.

Prof. Lineker

Installed at his hall, our hero set about using his powers of patronage. In 2016 he created a group of celebrity visiting fellows. These included Benedict 'Sherlock Holmes' Cumberbatch, Emma 'Hermione Granger' Watson, and a pop singer, Neil Tennant. All were opponents of Brexit. Was that why they were chosen? Or was the explanation more straightforward? Was it that other fellows at Lady

Margaret Hall were ferocious bores and Alan wanted
some stardust to make his high table rather less stodgy?
Three years later football's Gary Lineker was added to the
roll of honour. Was Lineker chosen for his distinction as a
pedlar of junk food, for his footballer's thighs and chest
or his ability to grab millions of pounds in pay from the
BBC? Again, it cannot be said Gary was a fervent supporter
of Brexit. But of course, low political orthodoxy –
subscription to a set of views rejected by the majority of
the electorate – can have had nothing to do with a scholastic honour. Can it? As ye sow, ye reap. In 2010, the
Guardian (editor: A. Rusbridger) urged its readers to vote
for the Liberal Democrats (leader: N. Clegg). Cleggy had
had 'a revelatory campaign'. The paper waxed poetic
about its 'enthusiastic' support for the yellow perils and
how their moment had come. Fast-forward a decade and
N. Clegg has become Sir Nicholas. Ejected from his parliamentary seat by the people of the Sheffield Hallam constituency, the former deputy prime minister was now coining
in millions as propaganda chief (sorry, 'vice president,
global affairs and communications') at Facebook, a
company until that point regarded by many liberals as
wicked. Facebook was going through a rough patch of
publicity, with all sort of accusations about its ruthless-
ness. Smart people were *getting* at it. And so the company
announced an international oversight board, a court of
world-respected leviathans, veritable Solomons. And who
should be on this committee of suitably remunerated
appointees? Dame Alan Rusbridger! Every saint's life has
its compensations.

The Trussell Trust, which campaigns in support of food banks, advertised a vacancy for a diversity and inclusion manager. The successful applicant would have 'the discipline to be able to clearly articulate complex concepts such as power, privilege, bias and intersectional injustice ... The ability to identify and realise shared "quick wins" that capture and signpost our direction of travel will be a distinct advantage.' The pay was £62,000. Think how many tins of beans that could buy.

Hot News

Bossy people tend to be pessimists. They think unless they are obeyed, the world will fall to pieces. Many are from the Left. The Left does not trust human ingenuity to improve our lot. It feels people must be kept in check by inspectors. Righties are less keen on regulation because it prevents them making a fast buck.

Climate activism has opened big territories to the world's tickers-off. It has given them a wonderful new realm for rules. They think it is possible to halt climatic change by preventing Western populations from consuming so much energy. This campaign allows the well-off to parade moral superiority while criticising others' consumption (cars, meaty diets, heating). In former ages that sort of position was reserved for monks and nuns. These modern postulants burn fervently against Agas. They become incandescent about light bulbs. Air travel makes them levitate. They say they have a right to interfere in our lives because there is no such thing as free choice. The type of heating system or motor car we select may, they say, have a bearing on whether or not the people of the Maldives stay dry. The moral certitude of this 'your compliance is my safety' argument is similar to that used by the Covid mask brigade.

The 2009 Richard Dimbleby lecture (by 'leaders of thought and action') was given by the Prince of Wales, whose household gobbles more kilowatts of energy than your average small town in Africa. The lecture was broadcast from a hot-looking room at St James's Palace and HRH, one of life's Eeyores, took climatic change as his subject. He calculated there were just ninety-six months left to stop irreversible damage to the world's climate. Armageddon's timekeeping may not be up to sniff, because in 2015 he returned to his lectern to announce that there were now thirty-five years left before we were doomed. Phew. The pressure was off for a while. And yet! In 2019, Charles had revisited his scribbled calculations and come up with a more doleful figure. He told Commonwealth worthies that he was 'firmly of the view' that they now had only eighteen months to come up with a solution to global warming or we'd had it. This sort of thing can be vexing for your average Noah. One moment he thinks he has more than three decades to build an ark. The next he is on an eighteen-month deadline. It's enough to make a shipwright yowl after whacking his thumb with a hammer.

When we lived near Stroud, Glos, there was a street preacher who shouted his stuff from the top of a pedestrianised shopping area. He was dressed in clothes that went out of common usage in the fifties. When you expect the world to end any moment, you possibly do not bother to refresh your wardrobe. With our two older children I would watch that preacher. He would brandish his Bible and proclaim his conviction that the Day of Judgement was nigh. I do not remember him putting quite such a precise dateline on things as Prince Charles did, but the message was the same: we must pull out of the decadent nosedive or we'd regret it. Whereas the heir to the throne is heard with hushed respect, the street preacher took some gyp. He was mocked by rougher Stroudies – shouts of 'Cheer up, granddad, it might never happen.' I admired that old man. He went out on his own in all weathers. He must have known that no one was really listening and yet he stuck to his principles. As for our two older children, they grew up thinking it perfectly normal to stand up in public, yelling at the wind. Their father at that time worked for the *Daily Telegraph*, after all.

We were just talking about medals and awards. Few people have won as many as the television producer and zoological populariser David Attenborough. His haul began with the Royal Geographical Society's Cherry Kearton Medal in 1972, a CBE in 1974, a BAFTA fellowship in 1980, the UNESCO Kalinga prize in 1981, his knighthood in 1985, acceptance into the Royal Victorian Order in 1991 and membership of the American Academy of Arts and Sciences that same year. There soon followed: the Kew International Medal, the Companionship of Honour, the International Cosmos Prize, the RSPB Medal, the Royal Society's Faraday Prize, the Descartes Prize, the Caird Medal and the World Cultural Council's José Vasconcelos World Award of Education. Who or what is the World Cultural Council? Answers in rhyming couplets, please. He had a flightless weevil and a ghost shrimp named after him. Next came the Order of Merit, the Nierenberg Prize, a special award from the National Television Awards, the Medal of the Institute of Ecology and Environmental Management, a British Icon Award, whatever that might be, plus the Peter Scott Memorial Award from the British Naturalists' Association, Fellowship of the Society of Antiquaries, a Progress Medal from the Royal Photographic Society (do recipients say 'snap' to one another?), a Prince of Asturias Award, the Fonseca Prize, the fair bonzer Queensland Museum Medal, the Founders' Medal of the Society for the History of Natural History, TV personality of the year from the Association for International Broadcasting, the IUCN Phillips Memorial Medal, Individual Peabody Award, Britain-Australia Society Award, Honorary Membership of the Moscow Society of Naturalists (you'd want to beware the Novichok soup at dinner), the Royal Canadian Geographical Society's Gold Medal, an Emmy Award, the Perfect World Foundation award, another Emmy, the Bodley Medal, a Landscape Institute Medal *avec* Fellowship, the World Economic Forum's smashing Crystal Award, another knighthood and, at the time of writing, thirty-two honorary degrees. Did he collect all these in person? If so, he must have left an enormous carbon footprint, but such are the burdens of secular sainthood.

Having belonged to a few judging panels, I can guess how some of these prizes came about. An obscure organisation craves publicity. It has a whizzo idea: let's give David Attenborough a prize and then the papers will all come and we will be briefly famous. But will he turn up in person? It's no use if he just records a video clip for the awards lunch. 'Well,' says a member of the judging panel, 'my cousin Bob plays golf with Attenborough's former agent's cousin and he might have an email address for him. We could offer decent expenses and accommodation at that posh hotel up the road.' And the amazing thing is, Sir David often said 'yes'. Why? Politeness? Vanity? Perhaps he is bored at home and likes going to hotels where they give you a chocolate mint on your pillow. But he does seem to be a right old tart for gongs.

TV wildlife presenter (left) and tortoise

Pre-beatification, Attenbore was a BBC suit. It is not such a big journey. There was a moment in the early 1970s when he might have become director-general of the Beeb, but instead he quit management and returned to programme making. Your career lasts longer as a creative. He made wildlife documentaries and was good at it. As he aged, he started to resemble that most noble of species, a tortoise. This only increased his appeal. Nor did it matter that – a deadly failing in other parts of broadcasting – he spoke in a pukka voice, because he was talking about animals and the British won't have a bad word said about an animal lover, unless he's Rolf Harris. By now Attenborough was a cherished figure but it was only when climate change became a middle-class activist issue that his secular canonisation was confirmed. He had already started to fancy his chances as a pooh-pooher of Christianity – he liked to say that it has simply 'never occurred' to him to believe in God, as though God was slightly non-U. He enjoyed the acclaim this won him with the atheist officer-class and followed it by taking what he called an 'engaged stance' on climate change. 'Engaged stance' means 'partisan'. This intrinsically BBC figure became a political campaigner. He waded into a planning row at Glyndebourne and campaigned for that opera house to be allowed to build a wind turbine on the South Downs. It was well away from his own home in Richmond upon Thames. He declared that human beings were 'a plague upon Earth'. In a move at odds with his support for human evolution, he appeared on a talk show presented by Jonathan Ross. Lots of other shows, too. As a buzzard hunts constantly for food, so does an Attenborough seldom turn down the chance of easy-meat publicity. When he granted an audience to President Obama at the White House, liberals were in heaven, if Sir David will forgive that expression. They discussed 'the future of the planet', two immortals on Olympus pondering mankind's destiny.

Was Sir David starting to become carried away by his own reputation? To seal his quasi-divine status, he and the Queen were filmed walking in the garden at Buckingham Palace and he took part in a slightly cloying stunt with the young Cambridge children, talking to them about monkeys and spiders. He gave Prince George, aged seven, a 23-million-year-old fossilised tooth. It was explained to the prince that the tooth came not from Sir David's gums but from a long-deceased shark. You needed a heart of stone not to laugh when the government of Malta said Attenborough had half-inched the fossil from that island in the 1960s, and maybe it was not his to give to the prince, after all. Then, oh then, came the cruel blow. After years of accepting invitations and backing causes and environmental rent-a-quotery, including celebrating the way that coronavirus had created a 'shared threat' for mankind so that we knew we were 'all in it together', he trod in a political cowpat. He demurred when Extinction Rebellion asked him for a supportive quotation. They were furious. How dare the old poot refuse to support their essential, planet-saving methods? XR Stormtroopers marched on Attenbore Towers in Richmond and protested outside, chanting and marching and knocking on his door, with Sir David, 94, staying inside, claiming he could not see them because he was scared of catching Covid off them. We weren't all in it together, after all.

When Russians force girls to become Olympic gymnasts, correct thinkers frown. When delinquent parents allow children to miss school for weeks, social services or the NSPCC intervene. But no one said a dicky bird when a pigtailed Swedish schoolgirl with depression issues, Asperger's syndrome, obsessive-compulsive disorder and selective mutism was hawked round the world as a champion of climate-change activism. Greta Tintin Eleonora Ernman Thunberg was soon as famous as her namesake Garbo. She may have wanted to be alone but her adult handlers weren't going to let that happen. No, siree. Not while Greta was hot news around the world and they could use her to pursue their political aims.

And the NSPCC never said a word

Greta complained that grown-ups were wrecking the planet for her generation. They should stop travelling, she said – in seven cities across the United States. They should not use so much energy, she said – under the arc lights of TV crews. Greta pouted. She pulled a cross face at Donald Trump, whoever he might have been. And from New Zealand to Alaska, Peru to Tokyo, adult politicians fought to adhere themselves to this moody little madam. In April 2019 she came to the House of Commons. John Bercow was still Speaker and you don't need me to tell you that that grotesque was soon pawing Greta, at least in the political sense. Bercow interrupted proceedings on the floor of the House to proclaim Greta's presence in the visitors' gallery. He held out one arm to her, Romeo serenading Juliet, and did a patronising little riff about how good it was to see 'young people' taking an interest in politics. How gracious it had been of Greta to visit him in Speaker's House and how fortunate he and other colleagues felt to have met her! Like sunflowers following the sun, we turned to look at the visitor. She sat there looking tremendously pissed off. Any amount of time spent with Bercow can do that to you, but the bubble-blowing glare on Greta's face was a humdinger. Bercow then announced the next piece of business 'urgent question, Mr Ed Miliband'. Greta fled. Wise before her years.

At the time of writing she is not yet eighteen, but she has already won almost as many awards as David Attenborough. She was named not only one of *Time* magazine's most influential teenagers (you shudder to think what the rest were like) but also one of its most influential people in the world. She was Swedish Woman of the Year, won the Fryshuset Scholarship, the Rachel Carson Prize, a Nobel Peace Prize nomination, a Goldene Kamera Award, the Fritt Ord Award, a papal Laduato si' Prize, an honorary doctorate from the University of Mons, an Amnesty International Ambassador of Conscience Award, a Gulbenkian Prize for Humanity (they're normally worth a million Euros), the Geddes Environmental Medal, an Honorary Fellowship by the Royal Scottish Geographical Society and a Right Livelihood Award. The keys to the city of Montreal were thrust in her tender hands by the mayor of Montreal, a woman with the commendably green name of Plante. Greta had a beetle and, perhaps less gratifyingly, a snail named after her. She was given the International Children's Peace Prize – children and peace hardly seem to mix – and *Forbes* adjudged her one of the world's 100 most influential women. *Glamour* made her its Woman of the Year. *Time*, determined not to be outdone and showing up *Glamour*'s appalling sexism, named her its Person of the Year. What a bunch of crawlers. But things backfired on the Nordic Council when it tried to give her its environment prize. Just as children will sometimes cross their arms and refuse to touch runner beans, Greta pushed out her lower lip and said she was going to have nothing to do with the valuable prize because Nordic countries were not doing enough to save Mother Earth. Greta's poor parents must have wept into their lentils that night, for the prize was worth 350,000 Danish krone, or about £42,000.

She had toured the world on what they called 'a sabbatical year'. She was, briefly, the big thing. Even the Greens' MP Caroline Lucas genuflected to her. But as the mayfly flutters and flops, so, perhaps, has Greta had her hour in the sun. Coronavirus arrived. The people of northern Europe, having long been told they should stop taking aeroplanes to their sunshine holidays, suddenly had no option but to stay at home. Wasn't much fun, was it? We were cooped up, unable to splurge, and we hated it. The end of the world really had arrived in one sense – the end of human fellowship and family gatherings, of freedom to roam and explore. The skies were empty of planes and it was . . . horrible. Extinction Rebellion was still up to its tricks but who cared? Eco-warriors had already started to lose public support when they tried to stop a crowd of early-morning blue-collar guys getting to work on the London Underground. That ended nastily with one prat being pulled off the roof of a Tube train. When lockdown happened, who cared if XR stopped the traffic and the trains? We were no longer going to work. The old boy in Stroud had been predicting Hell for years and now it was here. One hopes he felt at least a minor glow of 'told you so' satisfaction.

Saddle Soapsters

Inappropriate cycling without a helmet

Norman Tebbit was fed through the mincer after he told the 1981 Conservative Party conference that his unemployed father 'got on his bike and looked for work until he found it' in the Depression. For years Tebbit was attacked for an 'on yer bike' heartlessness. Yet today we are often told by politicians and officials and activists to get on our bikes and we are expected to admire the moral goodness – the zealful, liberal decency – of the message. Cycles are no longer an implement of oppression. They are chariots of rectitude. If you are less than blazingly ardent about them you may be dismissed as a rotten right-winger. Someone like Norman Tebbit.

As a boy I was devoted to my bicycle and would pedal busily around Cirencester, our home town, pretending to be James Hunt in his racing car. Riding up the hill to Somerford Road I would rumble my lips and make changing-down-gear noises like a Bedford lorry. More recently, on dry days, I have bumbled through central London on sturdy Boris bikes, without incident. Except once. It was morning and I was tootling along a bicycle path on The Mall, happily minding my own business, when a helmeted, Lycra-clothed maniac came up cycling fast behind me, panting. We were about 10 yards from a narrower, bollarded section of the path when Mr Lycra decided he needed to overtake me. He left it late and only just made it before we reached the bollards. 'F****** amateur!' he screamed. 'Get back in your car! C***suc*er!!!!' I was so taken aback, I nearly fell off.

Cycling once evoked thoughts of old maids weaving their way to evensong (or going rather faster if they thought randy John Major was in the laurel bushes). Cycling meant postmen squeaking down streets with a basket of parcels on their handlebars. Cycling was something done by Victorians in Sunday best, whiskered gents on penny-farthings, 1950s holidaymakers, provincial policemen, butchers' boys, chesty brunettes in *H&E* magazine, the Dutch royal family and the Goodies on their trandem. Cycling was benevolent, placid, and best when the going, though not your tyres, was flat. But somehow, at some point, it changed. The old innocence was replaced by something sweatier. Crosser. Helmeted. Oh, the bloody helmets. No longer was cycling a carefree activity with the wind blowing your locks. You were told, told and told again to wear a chin-strapped helmet that would stop you dashing out your brains when you had the inevitable crash. Helmets are not always such a great idea, or at least not on the ski slopes. Ask poor Michael Schumacher.

But back to cycles. Soon the early-morning streets were polluted by zooming twazzocks who thought they were Chris Hoy, bending over their racing bikes and going for the burn. The intensity was fetishistic and it was, one felt, done as a proclamation of virtue. If a pedestrian dawdled in the way, these racing demons swore viciously. In professional life they were probably bland nothings, anonymous toilers in the sausage-machine of office work, but on their bicycles they thought they ruled the world. I know some cyclists are considerate souls. But they would surely admit that plenty of their fellow saddle jockeys are crazily impatient, which may be an odd condition for people who have willingly chosen one of the slower forms of transport known to humanity. To the likes of Mr Lycra, cycling is not just about proceeding from A to B. It is not even about toning your calf muscles or saving a few bob in bus fares or doing your bit for the environment, all of which are creditable aims. Cycling has become an emotional signifier, semi-tribal, with all the fury about self-assertion and occupation of public spaces that was found in identitarianism. The accent is now on pedal *power* and it has become tyrannical. Not that Mr Lycra would like to be thought right-wing. He is more a middle-of-the-road hogger, often literally. Don't, what-ever you do, ask him to steer to one side or he will erupt. One of the latest manifestations of the cycle lobby's polit-ical machinations has been calls for a change to the Highway Code to scrap the old rules against riding two abreast. Cyclists want to be able to gum up the carriage-way, forcing motorists to dawdle behind them. Suck it up, Mr Toad.

Cycle lanes are, to today's city planners and transport wonks, what newly built urban churches were to the Victorians: emblems of spiritual progress. They allow progressive folk (e.g., Comrade Lycra) to assert control on the impure city. They allow mayors to demonstrate green credentials at other people's expense. Do cycle lanes cost millions of pounds? They do. But think of the reductions in CO_2 emissions, we are told. Do cycle lanes not cause worse traffic jams and therefore mean more vehicles are idling, causing more pollution? Well, yes. But eventually that will force motorists to give up cars in their frustration. Cycle lanes are being used to bend public behaviour and they are introduced with dishonest expressions such as 'reallocating road space'. That means 'taking road space away from cars'.

After Covid, the Department of Transport said it would spend £225 million to 'get Britain moving again'. This involved the blowing of millions of pounds on 'pop-up cycle lanes'. Demand for these lanes was not heavy. The *Daily Mail* found that in London, where £33 million was spent on a transport package including cycle lanes, just seven cyclists used a Euston Road cycle lane in a quarter of an hour. In the same period 420 cars chugged past. In Liverpool a busy stretch of road which had been narrowed to provide a cycle lane saw 300 cars versus two cyclists. Pavements were expanded, on the dubious grounds that pedestrians must not be allowed to brush close to one another in case they spread the plague. This caused further snagging of traffic in town centres, as did the introduction of more 20 mph zones. Bradford-on-Avon, Wilts, wasted £30,000 on one-way systems and pavement-widening 'to improve social distancing'. These caused gridlock. A quarter of the town's 10,000 population signed a protest petition. In our local city, Hereford, normal traffic was peremptorily banned from the old bridge over the Wye. Result: worse jams on the alternative bridge.

But who cares if motorists are inconvenienced? Our ruling class is determined to thrust eco-correctness on us all. Parking spaces were fenced off, losing local shops a fortune. Councils gaily spent cash on 'bike champions', free cycle lessons (are people really not able to teach themselves?) and 'Dr Bike' repair clinics. There was Bikeability training for youngsters teaching them how to 'assess traffic'. The government's transport department has devoted £2 billion of public money to cycling over five years. Two *billion*! That's a lot of puncture repair kits and 3-in-1 oil. Half a million £50 bike-repair vouchers were promised as part of the anti-Covid effort. Great dollops of public money go to Cycling UK, a charity that tells people to get on our bikes. Its patron is that well-known cyclist HM the Queen. Its president – a title possibly more to his taste – is the Channel 4 newsreader Jon Snow. Cycling UK is faultlessly right-on. When it promotes its Big Bike scheme it shows photographs of pretty young female mechanics. They did well to find some, because last time I popped into our local town's cycle shop, the repairs were being done by a couple of blokes with seventies rocker hairdos and not too many front teeth. Cycling UK also organises a Women in Cycling awards scheme which hails 100 'inspirational women helping others to experience the joy of cycling'. Joy? It is hard to believe they can really mean that when you read the Cycling UK website's detailed advice to memsahibs on how to advise saddle soreness. Are their vulvas 'innies' or 'outies'? Do they shave their down-belows?

Thank goodness I'm a chap (dread word).

Let's hope she read Cycling UK's advice on saddle soreness

Cycling UK may be a charity but its administrators look after themselves pretty well. Out of seventy-one staff in 2019, five were paid between £60,000 and £90,000. With total staff costs reaching £2.2 million, it spent £325,000 on its chief exec, its director of organisational effectiveness, its director of income generation, director of behaviour change and director of engagement and influence. Some of those job titles are pure Pyongyang. But how to keep hold of such juicy jobs? Simple. Start laying down the law. Become bossy. Make a nuisance of yourself. The charity's 'head of campaigns' assembled a slick package of advice to encourage members to take part in a mass write-in to parliamentarians and local newspapers in support of cycle lanes. The plan was to create the idea that cycle lanes had widespread support in the community. Do they?

A third of Cycling UK's moolah comes from grants from 'key partners and funders'. Its annual report lists thirty-six of these bodies. Nearly all of them are publicly funded bodies such as councils or other politically active charities which are themselves part-funded by the government. You thus have government money swishing round the system like water in a central-heating system, squirted from one public body to another in order to lobby, er, the government. Civil servants are paying a bureaucracy to lobby themselves; they can then present this to ministers as 'evidence' of public demand for the changes civil servants wanted in the first place but were worried about upsetting the public. Voters' money is used to engineer so-called evidence to do something the voters don't want.

The Third Sector (i.e., charities) has become a goitre on the body politic, feeding off public money in order to argue for yet more public money to be spent. In 2017/18, charities were given some £15 billion by national and local government. It is not easy to find out where it goes, but the Centre for Policy Studies think-tank found that the charities most generously funded by the government included the Royal Society for the Protection of Birds, the abortion-provider Marie Stopes International, Oxfam, Save the Children and the Wellcome Trust. The RSPB is understood to employ thirty-four press officers and have 685 members of staff who are fundraisers. In 2018 it was reported to have spent £57 million on 'fundraising, education and inspiring support' compared to £36 million on bird reserves. Oxfam has in the past attacked the government for not spending more of its money on aid (i.e., what Oxfam is supposed to do). Save the Children was one of the charities that whipped up support for footballer Marcus Rashford's attack on the Johnson government over free school meals. And the Wellcome Trust is the one that pays half a million quid a year to our friend Sir Jeremy Farrar, member of SAGE and Covid gloomster. How lovely to see our tax money being put to such good ends.

Before we pump up the old boneshaker's tyres for the homeward run, it may be worth examining the cycling/religion analogy a moment longer. Mr Lycra, when he came up on me that day I was cycling in London, was panting. His little legs, hard as steel pistons, were pumping up and down. He was sweating, his pulse pounding. He was punishing himself – a modern-day religious flagellant. Flagellation was a continental practice that came to England in 1349 when some 600 of its male practitioners arrived in London from Flanders. An Englishman, Sir Robert of Avesbury, described their antics:

> *They made two daily appearances wearing cloths from the thighs to the ankles but otherwise stripped bare. Each wore a cap and in his right hand had a scourge with three tails. Each tail had a knot and through the middle of it there were sometimes sharp nails fixed. They marched in a file one behind the other and whipped themselves with these scourges until they retired to their lodges. It is said that every night they performed the same penance.*

Two daily appearances? Militant cyclists do the same, rushing to and from work. A 'cap'? Helmet might be another word, just as a synonym for 'file' or 'pack' is the French *peloton*. Special clothes showing off the body? My dears, it was the fourteenth-century's answer to Lycra.

The National Distrust

Talking of which, down the street comes another file of middle-class fools flaying themselves and wailing about how dreadful we all are. These moping dolts are convinced we must repent. They lacerate their shoulders with thorn-tipped whips and plead forgiveness – simply so they can continue in their highly paid jobs and not be attacked by politico-terrorists. Ladies and gentlemen, it's the National Trust.

A few years ago, the Trust meant cream teas, week-end afternoon walks and Downton Abbey vistas. Its green car-windscreen sticker was as reliable an emblem of middle-bracket respectability as – once – was the antimacassar. Understated politeness, giving Gran a day out, Murray Mints in the glovebox of the Austin Maxi: those were the vibes. On the class scale it was below green gumboots but above shell suits. Today the National Trust is more likely to be associated with cultural self-anguish and obeisance to the grievance culture. Suffering! Disenfranchisement! Injustice! Another slice of Battenberg, Barbara?

'Unclean, unclean,' chants the leper in Leviticus, wearing 'a covering upon his upper lip', which may be the first historical reference to a face mask. That leprous unfortunate deserves our compassion, for he is bullied and picked over by (how typical) a priest. It is harder to feel pity for the National Trust's upper management. In 2019 the executive team of nine pocketed an average of £123,000. When these people chant 'unclean, unclean', they do so to burnish their own political credentials while making the rest of us feel bad about our forefathers. But we don't need them to do race politics or gay rights. We've got dear old David Lammy and Peter Tatchell for that. Had the original owners of those stately houses known the National Trust was going to disown them – and in the case of a shy High Sheriff of Norfolk, forty-eight years after his death, to out him as a friend of Dorothy – they might have sold their properties to the nearest spivvy developer, saying, 'Stuff this for a game of heritage soldiers.'

The National Trust for Places of Historic Interest or Natural Beauty (its full name) has become an industrial-grade incubator of revisionist race advocacy. It is not alone. The British Museum is riddled with this nonsense. Hartwig Fischer, its boss, went in for some institutional self-harm at the time of the Colson statue-toppling in Bristol, boasting about how he had moved a bust of the museum's founder, Hans Sloane, because Sloane owned slaves. 'We have pushed him off his pedestal,' said hot-to-trot Hartwig. 'Dedication to truthfulness when it comes to history is absolutely crucial.' Dedication to sponsors may be more important, mind you. The British Museum's website has a whole page gushing thanks to BP for being 'one of the museum's longest-standing corporate supporters'. There is no mention of BP's mottled corporate record as a polluter.

The National Trust writhes in embarrassment about its aristocratic properties. It aches to be thought matey. Scholastic precision has evaporated and illiterate signs proliferate. Visitors to Disraeli's Buckinghamshire house, Hughenden Manor, are told that 'Disraeli was very proud of his social climb' towards something called 'high soceity'. Makes you wash your eyeballs a bit, that typo, doesn't it? Notices, banners and posters have mushroomed, telling you about fun runs and kiddies' attractions and 'skills areas' and 'play areas'. Harry Mount, editor of the *Oldie* magazine, visited the Robert Adam house Osterley Park, west London, and was assailed by a vast banner hailing 'a new skills area for young families providing kids with a safe place to learn to cycle and gain confidence'. Children might have greater confidence without being nannied. Tony Berry, director of the Trust's Visitor Experience Department, inveighs against the 'outdated mansion experience'. He wants an 'audience-led approach', which moves away from art history and talk of aristocratic families and no longer regards stately homes as, er, homes. Instead, they should be 'repurposed as public space'. Berry scoffs at gardens being places of tranquil beauty. They should be used to lecture visitors, places where 'climate change can be acknowledged and tackled'.

Berry says change is needed because the Trust has a 'loyal but dwindling audience'. If it is dwindling, that may be because people are fed up with its political bellyaching. It ordered volunteers to wear rainbow lanyards to assert solidarity with LGBT rights. Did they think we might otherwise suspect these perfectly normal people of being anti-gay bigots? In 2018, white bags were placed over sculptures of men at one of the Trust's houses, Cragside in Northumberland, because it was trying to 'celebrate the role of women'. There was a row about the Trust dropping the historical-dating terms 'BC' (Before Christ) and 'AD' (Anno Domini) in favour of 'BCE' (Before Common Era) and 'CE' (Common Era) for fear of offending non-Christian visitors. Was anyone really offended?

Recent Trust obsessions have been women's rights, gay rights and environmentalism. Its current mania is the awfulness of the slave trade but that will change when fashion finds another cause. The Trust's mania for slavery has only flourished since it started trending on social media. Its contrition looks little more than opportunistic grovelling, done for the career convenience of senior managers. 'We're not here to make judgements about the past,' claims the Trust. Yes you are! 'No one alive today can ever be held responsible for the wrongs of the period when slavery took place,' it adds. So why beat us around the ears with all this slavery rubbish? The Trust's head curator, Sally-Ann Huxtable said: 'For me, now is a transformational time for the whole of society, and that includes the Trust.' At least she managed not to spell it 'soceity'.

After race protests in the summer of 2020, the National Trust issued an 'interim report' entitled 'Addressing our histories of colonialism and historic slavery'. That plural, 'histories', is something race advocates do to divide history into oppressors and victims. Here, in full, is how the interim report described the man who led our country during the fight against Hitler: 'Sir Winston Churchill (1874–1965), whose family home is Chartwell (NT), served as Secretary of State for the Colonies from 1921 to 1922. He was Prime Minister during the devastating Bengal Famine of 1943, the British response to which has been heavily criticised. Churchill opposed the Government of India Act in 1935, which granted India a degree of self-governance. On 1 July 1947, he wrote to Prime Minister Clement Attlee (1883–1967), arguing that India should not gain independence.'

The chairman of the National Trust was Tim Parker. Comrade Parker is not paid but he possibly does not need the money, having had a long career as a capitalist. Of the Trust's stately homes, he has observed that 'everything we have that is beautiful was almost certainly built by the exploitation of someone else'. That approach might have consistency if it came from a lifelong vegetarian Marxist. It is harder to take from someone who in his business career gained such a reputation for cutting that trades unionists called him 'the prince of darkness'. When Parker was at Clarks Shoes, he fired hundreds of employees. At Kwik-Fit he made £25 million for himself. He was once a Trotskyite, chaired the Oxford University Labour Club and worked under Denis Healey as a Treasury economist before discovering a belief in free enterprise just after Mrs Thatcher became prime minister.

Bendy sort of bloke.

Good Evening!

'And if you believe this old sausage rot,
you deserve me as your PM!'

September 22 2020: the government felt it had to up the
ante. Covid infection rates were rising and people were
enjoying themselves far too much. It was time to scare
the British public into obeying the rules. Time to remind
them who was in charge.

'Time for you to address the nation on television, Prime Minister,' murmured an adviser.

'Do you think so?'

'Nothing jolts them quite like an evening pep talk from their prime minister.'

'Am I that startling?'

'The public needs to hear from you, Prime Minister. This situation demands your personal authority. Your audience last time was triple that of *Coronation Street*.'

'Personal authority, ah yes. Rather. How many saw me last time?'

'Twenty-seven million.'

'I say! Sir Keir will be hopping.'

'I have booked the make-up artist, Prime Minister, and we have written your script. Perhaps a change of tie. The one you're wearing has custard on it.'

When prime ministers make televised addresses to the nation, it is generally a sign that:

a) There has been a cock-up.

b) The PM is *in die Fischsuppe*.

c) Other methods of communication having failed, Downing Street has decided to cut out the middleman and take its mouldering wares to the voters directly because they tend to be more generous-minded than Fleet Street or Parliament.

Boris Johnson duly did his Mr Eggy Eyes routine, earnest yet perky, at 8 p.m. that night, just as we were sitting down to beans on toast in front of the telly. He assured us he was 'deeply spiritually reluctant to infringe anyone's freedom'. Having said which, he slapped a curfew on pubs and restaurants, banned weddings with more than fifteen guests, and announced £200 fines for people who failed to wear masks, even if they were first-time offenders. Publicans who did not impose the mask rules on customers or staff would have to pay £10,000 fines. One publican I know makes barely that in a year. And yet our amiable premier, by fiat, was saying customers in pubs must not drink while standing and if they left their tables for so much as a moment they must wear masks. If they stood up maskless in order to place a new log on the fire or go to the loo – *wham*. They could be hit by a £200 fine and the landlord would pay fifty times that amount.

The Prime Minister: Our country is a freedom-loving country. If we look at the history of this country over the past 300 years, virtually every advance, from free speech to democracy, has come from this country. It is very difficult to ask the British population uniformly to obey guidelines. The way to do that is for us all to follow the guidelines which we will strictly enforce.

House of Commons, 22 September 2020

Translation: You Brits are disobedient buggers. I'm going to punish you until you bend.

The British public, hailed by Mr Johnson in parliament earlier that day as 'lovers of freedom', are also lovers of peace and quiet. They prefer not to have their evening leisure interrupted by a political crisis. Televised addresses by political leaders make us think of South American generals with Village People moustaches. Televised addresses start at Calais. Look at that popinjay Macron, surrounded by the brothel décor of the Élysée Palace. Televised addresses! Ronnie Barker got them to a T. 'Good evening,' says a plump figure with hands clasped. 'I'm squeaking to you tonight, once again, as the chairman of the loyal society for the prevention of pismronunciation'.

Harold Wilson's 'pound in your pocket' effort of November 1967 was an example. Wilson had been determined to avoid devaluing the pound. When the inevitable devaluation came, Wilson delayed the announcement until the Sunday newspapers' deadline had passed. He then made a Sunday-evening 'ministerial broadcast' to put his spin on the crisis. Look at Wilson's hands. The hands often speak more truth than the lips. Wilson, in that broadcast, does not know what to do with his hands. One moment he is clasping them, the next he fidgets and folds his arms. Then he brings them back in front of him and the fingers and thumbs twist and tangle. Richard Nixon solved the hands problem in his 1974 resignation broadcast by holding a script. Yet I still find his fingers bewitching: slender, the nails flawless, the fingers of an obsessive. Boris Johnson's hands, in his September 2020 televised address, were smeared in make-up.

Back to Harold Wilson in 1967. Sterling had fallen but housewives should not worry because 'the pound in your pocket or purse' was just the same value, and really this was a 'tremendous opportunity'. Today we would call this boosterism. Wilson talked of the government's 'duty' and its 'determination to win through' and of how we might 'solve our problems by our own exertions'. This was no time to apportion blame – no time to remind the viewers of the dockers and the seamen and the international currency speculators. Which of course he did. 'All of us together must now make a success of it,' said Wilson. We were all in it together. 'Do your bit, play your part,' said Matt Hancock.

The lies they tell. 'There are some in this country,' said a jowly Edward Heath in a 1973 broadcast, 'who fear that in going into Europe we shall in some way sacrifice independence and sovereignty. These fears, I need hardly say, are completely unjustified.' That 'I need hardly say' is a collector's item. One of the few regrettable things about Brexit is that Ted Heath did not live to see it. He'd have been *furious*. On a recent morning I came across an interview Heath gave about the 1973 gas workers' dispute. He spoke of the 'evolutionary process' and the 'stages' of the government's policies. 'We've been working very hard,' he said. That afternoon I heard Boris Johnson talk in the Commons about the 'stages' of the government's response to Covid, and I heard him say 'we've been working very hard'. 'There's just one thing that drives me,' said David Cameron in his televised New Year's message in 2016, 'and that is what is best for the national interest.' They nearly always say something like that. Nixon said it in 1974. Boris invariably says it. Cameron gave a homily about the importance of our voting to stay in the EU, but added that he was working hard to get a great new deal with Brussels. What a shiny-chinned fibber he was.

During the Brexit terrors, Theresa May did several televised addresses. At one point she was on the box more than Holly Willoughby. Mrs May assured us she was 'on your side' on Brexit. Untrue. She was on her own side, thrashing around like a crane fly in a cobweb. The end came. Anthony Eden was similarly doomed when, during Suez in 1956, he made a nine-minute televised address from a stuffy BBC studio. He was convinced the Beeb engineers tried to unsettle him by shining lights in his eyes after making him climb a long flight of stairs. Agents of Nasser, no doubt. Eden talked about how he was 'a man of peace'. He added, 'I was a League of Nations man', as if that helped. Suez blew up in his face, finishing the British Empire, not because Eden had been a man of peace but because he had been recklessly bellicose. If you watch the broadcast you will see that at the end of his broadcast Eden says, 'Good night to you all,' and then leans back, quite drained. The camera stays on him just long enough to catch him licking the upper front-inside of his lips. It is a telling moment, catching his dry-mouthed exhaustion. A few weeks later he was replaced by Harold Macmillan, who, although not a natural on television, was drawn to its flame. Macmillan wiggled those begging eyebrows and said we were all going to face 'a difficult task'. Prime ministers love telling us we are all going to have to 'work hard' and 'be determined' and show our British grit. Why should we? We elect them to do the work. They volunteer for it. We don't. They talk of the country 'striving' and of national 'determination' in order to impart shared morality to their personal dilemmas. They hope to shame us into thinking that we are some-how to blame for their balls-ups and pratfalls.

In March 2003, Tony Blair burst into our evening

viewing to tell us that the Iraq War had begun and British service personnel were at that very hour in action. Actually, Blair recorded the broadcast in advance, so he was not being strictly truthful. What a surprise. The mission, said Blair with butch briskness, was 'to remove Saddam 'Ussain and disarm Iraq of its weapons of mass destruction'. As he said that he did an unusual amount of blinking. Only later would we discover that no weapons of mass destruction were found. Blair argued that but for the allies' attack, the world faced 'disorder and chaos' and terrorists did not care for 'the sanctity of human life'. As the shot closed in on his youthful face, he averred that removing Saddam would be 'a blessing to the Iraqi people'. It was a slick performance, melding saintliness and aggression. You could almost sense the adrenalin pumping through his gonads. How artfully rehearsed it all was, with the little jinks of his head. 'Disorder and chaos' were, alas, exactly what his war caused.

Normal people take holidays. Bossocrats take 'annual leave'. They take this 'annual leave' more than once a year. Leave was a term reserved for members of the armed forces. Now you receive an email from a minor council menial saying, 'I am away on annual leave. If your email is urgent, please contact my PA on the following number.' Translation: 'My job is a prosaic, desk-bound affair but I am more important than you.'

If You've Time to Spare,
Travel by Air

Airports were into bossy misery long before Covid-19. Just as the early aviators were pioneers, taking to the skies in machines made from kindling, chewing gum and catgut, the likes of Heathrow and Gatwick were among the first to make life hell for customers. Flying as a sybaritic experience was ditched. For hassle and general embuggerance, air travel was soon in a class of its own. The BOAC shoulder bags and pre-flight café crèmes gave way to budget airline price-trickery and franchise branches of Burger King in a leaky departures hall. Airport managers were in their element.

Passengers shuffled in queues like Guantanamo Bay prison inmates waiting for their evening slop. Prohibitions abounded. Scanning machines stripped you to your smalls, giving the operating staff a good laugh. 'STRICTLY CREW ONLY' notices put you in your place and boarding gates were half a mile away. Walking to them, you'd pass old ladies whose bones had given up on them on the Long March and had been abandoned like lorries on the road to Basra. When you tried to buy a packet of wine gums at the shop you were told to produce a boarding pass. Why? So that those chiselling bastards at WHSmith could reclaim the VAT. The lounges seldom had enough free seats. Of course not. Passengers should go and sit in the 'food outlets' and spend money. Then there were the delays, late take-offs, blithe cancellations, announced nonchalantly by an industry that cared little. Is it any wonder the public failed to rally to the cause of another runway at Heathrow?

Airlines start telling you off the moment you book a flight. You are instructed to fill in your passport details and if you accidentally insert a capital O instead of a numerical 0 you will be whacked with a surcharge at the airport or banned from boarding the flight. You must promise not to pack a gas canister or hand grenade. The spoilsports! Leave your Colt .45 at home. Do we ever have a 'please'? Travelators (very much an airport word) with metallic voices instruct you where and how to stand. Mirthless gate goons check your passport for the umpteenth time and glower if you hold it upside down or if your row of seats has not yet been summoned. Maybe you were unable to understand the deafening BING-BONG announcement that was made in such a bored, formulaic, singsong manner. When the cabin crew do finally greet you at the door of the aircraft to say, 'Welcome aboard,' what they really mean is, 'You poor sods, we know what you've just been through and you look as if you need a drink.' At last, after the interminable slamming of overhead lockers, you can sit for an hour or so – and, yes, maybe sink a couple of large gins, if the drinks trolley reaches you in time because now they have to charge everyone for even a cardboard beaker of coffee and it takes ages to grab everyone's money. You have just about recovered your equilibrium when it is time to tackle the stinky-bogged airport at the other end.

To be an airport manager is to be a controller of people, not their servant or facilitator. It is to be an abattoir hand, steering cows through pens. Passengers are not voyagers in need of swift transit or clients whose patronage is valued. They are a problem to be processed and, if we can bend the abattoir analogy, milked. Squeeze the herd's wallets. Relieve them of (on average, according to a 2015 survey) £52 a head of their holiday spending money. Passengers aged 25–34 spent more – an average of £82. Airports suck up that cash not by accident. They design that unavoidable path through the duty-free shopping area in such a windy way that we have to walk past twice as many displays of overpriced liqueurs as we might otherwise have done. Sales assistants squirt clouds of not-so-heavenly scent until you feel you are at the Battle of the Somme during a mustard-gas attack. Control the herd. Monetise! Maximise profits!

Intimidation is part of the equation. They make passengers feel small so that they spend in an act of defiance, trying to make their families look up to them. From the moment you arrive at an airport, you are told off. And charged. Birmingham Airport demands £3 for 15 minutes if you wish to drop off friends at its door. What other business imposes a fee on customers simply for arriving? This is 'to maintain visitor safety'. Ah, the old 'safety' gambit. 'If you see areas designated as Red Routes you are not allowed to stop, unload or park, even if you are just dropping off passengers. Use the Drop Off car park instead.' Translation: there's no escaping our exorbitant and mean-minded drop-off fee. Don't you even think about pulling up on that pavement for 30 seconds to drop Grandma and her bags. To lend the whole thing an extra aura of bossy menace, the airport adds: 'We operate a vehicle monitoring and enforcement operation. Any vehicle flouting the Red Route restrictions will face an enforcement charge of £100.'

Airport managers are the senior figures in this relationship. You, the passengers, are pond life. The airports rule. You queue at a machine to deposit the luggage which has already cost you several quid a bag. You collect the pre-booked seat number which sets you back a few more jimmies. You must then join another wait for the security checks, unless you have thrown some baksheesh at these bandits for their 'express' lane. You are frisked. You are squirted up the jacksy with high-jet air which allegedly will establish whether or not you have touched gunpowder in the last few hours. No, I haven't. But had I known what an unpleasant experience this was going to be, I might well have brought my atom bomb. You are told to stand behind the yellow line and wait behind one of those security cordons with the flimsy lightweight metal poles. This is under the arbitrary sway of bored employees in nylon uniform and spongy shoes, their names illegible behind the scuffed laminate of an ID lanyard provided by some logistic-solutions company run from an industrial estate outside Tipton by shysters on six-figure bonuses. Does anyone ever check these security guards? How hard would it be for a terrorist to get work as an airport guard?

Meanwhile, there is a query over your hand luggage. Alarm bells honk, lights flash and a canned voice says

'Attention! Attention!', as if someone has jumped over the Berlin Wall. Your spongebag is sent down a chute reserved for the effects of al-Qaeda killers. Fellow passengers – it has already been three hours since most of them left home – watch you with the haggard pity of factory-farmed sheep who have seen one of their number dragged away to be given an electric bolt through its brains. 'This your bag?' grunts an operative, wearing the latex gloves doctors use when they are about to stick a finger up your fundament. 'Yes,' you gulp. 'Open it, please, sir!' It takes months of practice to perfect that tone of sneering contempt. 'What's in here?' 'My packed lunch.' You dread him unwrapping that squashy little oblong in the silver foil. There is no knowing what might happen if he puts that through his gelignite detection machine. 'What is this? Drugs? Contraband?' Actually, it's my fish-paste bap. Would you like a bite?

Paws for Thought

Is she about to strangle that dog?

Back to dogs for a moment. The Richmond Park atrocity mentioned by Flip in her Foreword would not have happened had Fenton been sent to Barbara Woodhouse. Mrs Woodhouse (1910–1988) was a dog trainer who loved hitting the T in 'siTTT!' Her other catchphrase was 'walkies', delivered in a tone of girlish excitement. For years she ran kennels but in 1980 she was given a BBC TV series and became a star. She was a blissful creation: sensible skirts, a bagful of teeth, maybe just the slightest whiff of the cork. She treated people much as she did dogs, bossiness alleviated by pukka distraction. Engaging eccentric or a strident sergeant major? Both.

Training for police dogs is important. I will give you that. But does it really matter if your friend Tiddles 'siTTTs' when told? Declaration of interest: I have two untrainable terriers who would have gnawed Barbara Woodhouse's ankles and soon found themselves on the wrong end of her brogues. Our dogs have, in the past, been in trouble with the constabulary. A policeman drove out from Hereford after one of them sampled a passing jogger's lower leg. We do not often see police in our part of the county. Tractors speed down the lanes, thieves pinch garden furniture, fly-tippers dump sofas in fields and the police do bugger all. But a small terrier gives a bearded jogger a nip after he strayed off the footpath on to our garden and nee-naw-nee-naw, Plod is on the case, hastening to the scene of the crime like Kojak with his red light on the sedan roof. The copper himself claimed to be nervous about dogs and entered our house holding a canister of anti-dog spray. If he was that scared of a terrier, you slightly wondered how much use he would be against cosh-wielding bank robbers. He admitted that our dog seemed harmless but I had to sign some piece of paper saying we would try to ensure she never nipped another old fool in running shorts.

Looking at what has happened in Britain in the past few months, you could say that our politicians and officials have gone a bit Barbara Woodhouse. They have become obsessed with trying to impose obedience, forcing us to 'siTTT' at home much of the time and to take 'walkies' only with our household bubbles. The one difference with Mrs Woodhouse was that she was above all else a dog lover. She believed there was 'no such thing as a bad dog'. She possibly preferred dogs to humans. Officialdom is less benign. It seldom thinks 'there is no such thing as a bad citizen'. There is a nagging suspicion that much of the crapola we have had to endure recently was done not so much for our own good but for the benefit of those giving the orders. Barbara Woodhouse may have been an imperious old trout but she was basically on the dogs' side.

Inclusion Via Exclusion

Next time they award Best Picture at the Oscars, it will need an asterisk. Best Picture*. And underneath: '*according to our quotas'. Films will not be judged on merit. Something else – our old friend Herr Finger-Wagger – has intervened. In September 2020 the Academy of Motion Picture Arts and Sciences introduced quota demands for films. In future they would only be eligible for an Oscar if at least one lead character was from an 'underrepresented racial or ethnic group'. At least 30 per cent of the ensemble cast must be from at least two under-represented groups (women, racial, ethnic, LGBTQ+, or people with disabilities); or the film must be about one of those groups. There must be similar minority involvement on the other side of the camera, from the film-set crew to studio department chiefs, distributors' apprentices and in the marketing and publicity departments.

Your film – about, say, the Manchester United air crash, or Captain Scott's polar expedition or Donald Trump's crazy gang – has a white, able-bodied, male cast which is less than 30 per cent 'under-represented' groups? Sorry, unless you insert a gay subplot involving Matt

Busby and one of the lads, or invent a scene in which Captain Oates bumps into some female Inuit, or put Steve Bannon in a wheelchair and make Mike Pence wear a white stick and callipers, your movie cannot be considered for our awards. Maybe your distribution boss, a Hispanic woman, has unexpectedly quit to join a rival company. As a result of her departure, the quota percentage drops below the crucial level. There goes the clank of the bog chain as your film, which was considered a runner for an Oscar, is ruled ineligible. How clever of your rivals to headhunt the distribution boss at the killer moment. Once the ceremony is over, they can sack her and still have made a financial profit because their film won the prize instead.

Political interference in Hollywood was tried in the 1950s by J. Edgar Hoover. It remains a bad idea. Olivier's *Hamlet* would not have made the quotas cut. Ditto *Platoon*, directed by that liberal Oliver Stone. *The Italian Job*: do Italians count as BAME? If so, we may need more shots of the Turin traffic cops in order to hit the 30 per cent target. Ditto any films about the Mafia, though of course we must not besmirch anyone with casual stereotyping of Italian-Americans. Bobby de Niro and da boys may need to rein in their accents. We can probably kiss goodbye to any Oscar-winning biopics about Clement Attlee or – next best thing – Vladimir Putin, or most American astronauts, or motor racing pre-Lewis Hamilton. Samuel Beckett's *Waiting for Godot* looks less of a runner, unless Vladimir or Estragon can become an Algerian. Lucky, be a lady tonight. Anyone writing a film treatment of Solzhenitsyn's *One Day in the*

Life of Ivan Denisovich can replace the pen top. Nor do things look good for dramatisations about Irish Republicanism or Shakespeare's theatrical company or the Vatican.

The academy, telling its 9,000 members they must undergo unconscious bias training, certainly had a political problem. Its previous awards ceremonies had been remarkably light on people of colour. The new rules were announced at the height of the Black Lives Matter anguish. Here was an institution panicking in the face of violent protest, saving its own white bottoms by ditching principle. When art awards are used for political posing, they lose their truthfulness. At what point does the British Board of Film Classification intervene to advise cinema customers that the film they are about to watch was made without due regard to quotas? At what point is the freedom of filmgoers to make their own decisions interrupted by monitors who think they know better?

British cinema is not immune from this. BAFTA elected its first BAME chairman, Krishnendu Majumdar, a little-known film producer. He took it upon himself to write to all BAFTA members. Remember: this man is meant to be a tribune for some of our most brilliant and creative minds. Here, in a markedly shortened version, is what he said:

> *I'd like to share some thoughts on my personal journey. I was never the likeliest candidate. My father was an Indian immigrant who settled in the South Wales valleys as a GP. Growing up, there was no one from the Bengali community with connections in the film or television industries. We can*

evolve. My election shows that at this defining hour, change is possible in this venerable institution.

We are a global community and I want to make sure we are there for all of you. I don't want to leave anyone behind.

I take on this role at a critical point in modern history. The horrific killing of George Floyd has ignited huge waves of anti-racist demonstrations. I feel that every organisation, including BAFTA, must play its role responding to this movement.

Racism and structural inequality are ingrained in society. It's important that we don't just acknowledge overt racism and verbal barbs – it is also crucial that we talk about the unseen, insidious, systemic racism. Everything leaves a psychological toll.

We're at a crossroads for society.

It is now up to us – as a society, as an industry, as an organisation, as individuals – to rise to the challenge. We all have to do the honest, uncomfortable work of rooting out racism. Organisations can no longer stand back from societal issues.

For me, the 2020 Film Awards nominations earlier this year highlighted some uncomfortable truths for BAFTA and represents its own moment of reckoning. The awards are an indicator of how we are progressing. It is right that we have accepted responsibility for this, and that we have announced an immediate and wide-ranging review into the awards – which I am personally leading.

I can tell you, without doubt, that this review is one of the most important steps BAFTA has undertaken in recent years. We have never opened ourselves up like this before.

It has been an important part of our growth as an organisation. We are listening. We are hearing many opinions on where we have fallen short. This has been an instructive part of our learning process.

We should never become complacent.

I believe these nominations can act as early markers on our journey.

Together we can make a difference. I look forward to embarking on this journey with you. Bring it on.

Best,

Krish

Krish the krashing bore.

Harry Kari

Harry Wales: left, left, left, left, left

Not since Saul of Tarsus walked to Damascus has there been such a conversion. Prince Harry, freest of spirits, Hal for our days, a rip-snorting, hog-whimpering, pheasant-bagging arm-farter, has been pasteurised. Denuked. Colonised. He has been turned into a preachy wokester who now lives in Santa Barbara amid the facelifts and shrivelled dewlaps of celebritydom. Poor lad. Might he and the pup Archie not soon start an escape committee?

Original Harry was full of beans. He was the sort of six-year-old who bounds up to you, fists flailing, and you hold your palm against his head to keep him at a distance while he keeps boxing. Original Harry was the non-intellectual one with the wooden rifle and kid's soldier-uniform, a full head of red hair and a sporran of oats. We ached for him when his mother died in 1997 and, days short of his thirteenth birthday, he had to walk behind her horse-drawn coffin. That could have been the moment he crumpled, but he found a girlfriend, Chelsey Davey, who was cigs and gins and a Sid James laugh, and he sucked down British ale like a fire engine's extraction hose. Harry liked strip billiards. When photographed starkers in Las Vegas with some boobalicious babe (not Chelsey), he did not seem specially fazed. Nor were the British people. A few prudes took umbrage and Buckingham Palace fretted but most of us cut him a gusset. Original Harry tried dope – who hasn't? – and was said to clobber the occasional over-intrusive paparazzo outside London nightclubs. Worse things happen.

Harry joined the Army and occasionally succumbed to barracks language. He would not have passed muster in the leader-writers' room at *Prospect* magazine. Instead, against the wishes of some courtiers, he went to Afghanistan and fought for Grandmother and country. He attended Twickenham rugby matches wearing an England shirt, with a new, dreamy girl on his arm and a beer in hand. Original Harry wore silly outfits to fancy-dress parties. Rather him than me. Into the room would come his pal Guy Pelly dressed as Shirley Bassey, and Harry, knocking back a tinny, would do the nose trick. He was not, nor is yet, one of life's Radio 3 listeners. He was photographed in scuffed combat boots and desert fatigues with an ID chain round his neck. He could strip a machine gun and fly a helicopter – so not a complete fool. He could gallop on a polo pony. He was a blood and a blade. Harry was good for morale.

All that has gone. The waistline is leaner and so is the personality. It happened after his marriage to Meghan Markle, divorced, American TV actress, professional emoter. She was a small notch above Harry intellectually but they seemed a good match. Some sneered that it would never last; I confess I liked Meghan. As a couple they looked pretty sporty. Windsor was *en fête* for their wedding in May 2018. The sun shone. Crowds came out in their thousands. Meghan's mother was a portrait of dignity. The bride herself had poise and beauty. Music: Elgar, Holst, Warlock, one slightly drippy hymn ('Lord of All Hopefulness') and one solidly Welsh ('Guide Me O Thou Great Redeemer'), some gospel singing to mark the African-American connection and wonderful cello from Sheku Kanneh-Mason. But the sermon was a worry. The sermon was the giveaway. Meghan had become an Anglican, christened by the Archbishop of Canterbury. His Grace was on parade and would surely have been happy to do the preaching honours but he failed to catch the selector's eye. Meghan had flown in an American bishop, Michael Curry. What a show-off. What a Mr

Windy. He went on and on and on and on. After a quota-tion from the Book of Solomon, bang, he was straight into some Martin Luther King, sure to make posh whiteys feel on the back foot. And then Curry told them not to over-sentimentalise love.

Over-sentimentalisation is not, by and large, a British failing, but it was certainly something to which the bishop himself was prone. Love was 'power, real power, the power to change the world', he warbled. He crouched at the lectern like Franz Klammer entering a slalom gate, over-projecting, overdoing it. He twisted at the waist. He threw his head left, right and high and low, thrashing around for attention, a terrier trying to kill a rabbit. He popped his eyes and gave it bags of Bisto. What a ham. And there was Harry, listening with a faintly glassy eye, possibly not copping everything the Sky Pilot was saying but quietly complimenting himself on having landed himself a peacherino of a bride – and maybe worrying what his old mucker Pelly had got up to in the wedding-night pranks department.

By now the bishop was sawing away with his arms, declaring that 'love is not selfish and self-centred'. Unlike you, mate. The congregation, which included the Beckhams and the Clooneys and Oprah Winfrey and that paragon of marital fidelity Sir John Major, was instructed to imagine love so transforming the world that 'no child will go to bed hungry in this world ever again'. Not a single child. Ever. Anywhere. All from love? Come off it, Curry. 'We will let justice roll down like a mighty stream!' honked the prelate, 'and righteousness like an ever-flowing brook. Where love is the way, poverty will become history. We will lay down our swords and our shields, down by the riverside, to study war no more.' Both the groom and his best man were dressed in frockcoats of the Blues and Royals, a cavalry regiment. Units lending their dash to the wedding parade included the Royal Marines, 3 Regiment Army Air Corps, the Royal Gurkha Rifles and the band of the Irish Guards. Down to the Thames, pronto, lads and throw your epaulettes into the river. The padre's just declared unilateral disarmament.

On and on this preacher went, slipping in a mention of the slaves in the old antebellum South. Prince Harry, by now, was starting to look anaesthetised. His jaw was swinging at the hinges. The Duchess of Cambridge gave a not entirely loyal smirk. Watches were being discreetly consulted and a certain amount of coughing had begun. But Curry was not to be denied his moment in the spotlight. The world was watching and he was going to make himself famous. He diverted into a mini-lecture about a Jesuit scholar, Pierre Teilhard de Chardin, and his theory that fire was the greatest discovery ever made by mankind. What the congregation now longed for was a flame-thrower to set light to the Rt Rev. Chatty Man's sermon notes. That pebble-grinding groan from near the high altar? Prince Philip gnashing his dentures. The Queen shot one of her Hanoverian glares at the middle distance. Curry was mentioning migration and the internet and, once more, Dr King. Time now, please.

Bishop Curry got what he wanted. Many of the head-lines next day were about him. He had barged himself into an English royal wedding and he had been suffi-ciently sharp-elbowed for anti-Royalists to lap it up, even though they would not normally have much time for a bishop's puckerings. Six months later Curry published a book of his sermons (£14.99) entitled *The Power of Love*.

When the Sussexes, as they became, began married life, it was soon apparent that the new duchess was going to follow the Curry approach by being indignantly American in her approach. She expected others to bend to her aesthetic. She was appalled when her synthetic effusions were not applauded. She made mileage of her minority-ethnic background. The daughter-in-law of the heir to the Throne was playing the victim card. Courtiers apparently failed to make the right noises. Rancour mushroomed. There were allegations of snubs and rudeness to Meghan by other royals. Families can be like that: an omitted compliment soon becomes a vicious slur, at least in the imagination of a newcomer. There were hints of anti-American and anti-black prejudice. Maybe Meghan was tricky. Then came the lectures about climate change and mental health. And the hideously self-pitying Oprah interview.

Once-carefree Harry, Captain of Burps, kept furrowing his brow, though not because he was suppressing another belch. He was frowning because he wanted us to know it wasn't easy. Life was hard. He, in his princely cocoon, felt our pain. The climate-change homilies were particularly hard to swallow because the couple continued to use private jets. They said they would be dumping their royal connections, yet called their new website Sussexroyal.com. They promoted democratic engagement – recording a get-out-the-vote video which was pretty clearly a 'vote for Biden' message – yet their own prominence flowed entirely from the non-democratic institution of the British monarchy. They posed as saints of self-denial and said they were going to try to become financially independent while they were splurging vast sums on a new house in California. They attacked the press for intrusion yet were more than happy when cameras caught them giving food to the needy. Did Herself cooperate with *Finding Freedom*, that fawning biography about her and Harry? How did that sit with her demands for privacy? She and Harry announced they had 'chosen to make a transition' and would be 'carving out a new role'. This was alongside a statement that the duke would be retaining the rank of major and the honorary ranks of lieutenant commander and squadron leader. What about strolling down to the waterside to lay down our swords and shields? For Remembrance Day 2020, British congregations stood in the rain at local war memorials to remember the fallen. Meghan and Harry tried to muscle in on things by making a staged visit to a graveyard in California. It was all about them. Look at us in our masks, grief as a fashion choice, adopting a pose for our own self-glorification. The stunt backfired. Meghan's response was to hire two more PR advisers. More manipulation. More messaging. The nation pressed 'unsubscribe'.

The Sussexes were not alone in their climate-change jet-setting hypocrisy. Cardiff University analysed the travel habits of scientists. Its study was published in Global Environmental Change and was based on answers from fifty-nine countries. Which group of researchers took the most airline flights? Those engaged in climate science.

They've Got an A-Gender

*Enoch urges a doubtful audience to challenge
normative structures of gender and sexuality*

London's School of Oriental and African Studies, founded
in 1916 to teach colonial administrators, is not what it
was. Enoch Powell went there to learn Urdu in the hope
that it would equip him to become viceroy of India (he
didn't). Missionaries and administrators with the Imperial
Civil Service studied law and customs in dusty parts.
Language teaching, from Amharic to Yoruba, was the
focus. Today's SOAS, as it is now known, is a different

affair. Languages are still offered, but where once the emphasis was on preparing Western bureaucrats and businessmen for Africa and the Orient, now it is about asserting minority identities in British political culture and in coaching African and Asian 'thought leaders' in Western political norms.

Learning a language is hard. Attending a November 2020 one-day festival showcasing 'multilingual London', celebrating the 'vibrant' languages spoken in the capital, is a little easier. 'Join us for a day of performances, artistic interventions, panel discussions and writers' talks' said the publicity for this SOAS event. One 'exciting session' was about exile; another was about how 'languages in families can set up barriers or create secret idioms'. Exiles, barriers: why so negative? Are languages not an opportunity? The festival was funded by the European Research Council under the European Union's 2020 research and innovation programme. Britain had left the EU ten months earlier.

SOAS also announced the Ebony Initiative, 'to increase the pipeline of black scholars progressing to academic positions in UK higher education'. It explained, in jargon that almost needed its own translation aid, that 'this faculty-initiated programme takes a multi-pronged approach which includes academic skills building sessions, community building spaces, career mentoring and funding support and guidance'. Althea-Maria Rivas, 'lecturer in development studies and lead co-ordinator of the Ebony Initiative' said it would 'recognise the importance' of 'racialised students'. Racialised? What does that mean? Do they have a word for it in Pashto or Hittite? British colleges needed 'to recognise that the institutional racism and structural obstacles black students are struggling against in UK universities must be addressed as a matter of urgency'.

In that 'need to' and 'must' there is a stridency which jars in an academic prospectus, not least one offered by an institution that pockets millions of pounds of public money. Has SOAS lost the pioneering individualism its earliest students had? It certainly doesn't seem terribly keen on box wallahs these days. The school's career service held three fairs for employers and job seekers. These concentrated on job openings in volunteering, the Law, and the public sector/charities. There was no fair for commerce or manufacturing.

Despite its large bung from the taxpayer, SOAS is struggling. You might have thought that Asian language-teaching would be a growth area in a post-Brexit Britain. My son took himself off to China to learn Mandarin. From him I know that the Asian language sector is surging. If SOAS concentrated on that, equipping our young-sters for trade abroad, it might be on to something. But it is more keen on social and political lecturing. The school has a Centre for Gender Studies which is described thus:

An interdisciplinary space promoting research and teach-ing on Gender with particular reference to Asia, Africa and the Middle East, and their diasporas. CGS has become a hub of research and training, working to support anti-racist fem-inisms and social movement challenging normative construc-tions of gender and sexuality. Our focus on Asia, Africa and the Middle East productively disrupts the teleologies of

181

'Western' feminism and our critical study of Europe and its 'others' has earned us a reputation as a fertile seedbed for queer and trans thoughts, transnational feminisms, critical legal theory and anti-racist knowledge production. Grappling with the legacy of SOAS as a training ground for the administrators of Anglophone Empires, at CGS we not only tackle the long complex entanglements of modern feminisms with white imperialism and postcolonial nationalisms, we also incubate new strategies to decolonise feminist scholarship and praxis.

You're not getting off that lightly. There is more . . .

Offering a suite of MA Programmes, Postgraduate Research Degrees, Online Postgraduate Degrees and Short Summer Courses, CGS at SOAS stands at the cutting edge of postgraduate education for the next generation of change makers with new visions for feminist futures. Drawing annual cohorts of students who have received a wide range of disciplinary training in their undergraduate years in both Global South and Global North contexts, CGS cultivates a unique interdisciplinary space committed to forging connections between feminist scholarship and activism.

Teleologies, praxis, Global North contexts . . . if only Enoch had chosen to become fluent in this gibberish rather than boring old Urdu, he might have become a modern 'change maker' rather than being written off as a rotten old white supremacist. The chancellor of SOAS, by the way, is the Princess Royal. Wonder what she makes of it all.

Bossiness is not the same as rudeness. Bossiness is actually at its most bloody annoying when it is simperingly considerate. Norman Balon ran the Coach and Horses pub in London's Soho and was 'London's rudest landlord'. His memoirs were entitled 'You're barred, you bastards!' But Norman wasn't bossy. When a bunch of Hoorays turned up at the Coach and demanded pints of snakebite, Norman replied: 'We don't serve cocktails. Piss off.' Willie Hamilton MP, socialist critic of the Royal Family, arrived for a *Private Eye* lunch upstairs. 'Hey, you, where are the stairs?'

Norman, taking against Hamilton's tone, told him to eff off. The MP gasped that he had never been spoken to like that in his life and departed in a huff. When the *Eye* lunch heard of this, everyone cheered.

Press Squeezed

Here I am, a newspaper hack, inveighing against bossiness, yet newspapers themselves are not averse to comment articles with the word 'must'. My old paper, the *Daily Mail*, enjoyed whipping out the megaphone. My current employer, *The Times*, was known as 'The Thunderer' and still has a column called that. The *Guardian* may think itself open-minded but it can be just as strident as the *People's Banner* in the novels of Trollope. Its cunning editor, Mr Quintus Slide, used sanctimony to wound political foes. Slide lives.

In a 1948 book, *46 Not Out*, the late cricket correspondent R. C. Robertson-Glasgow wrote:

> *No Editor, even if four out of his eight pages exhibit little else but potted pictorial sex, is wholly free from the idea that he must teach his readers what they ought to think. He knows, and they know, that they don't want to think. They've had enough thought on whether Arsenal can beat Chelsea. But he sticks to it, does the Editor. He slips in an occasional leading article on Bessarabia or Calories; that's for education and the look of the thing. Then he hits on that perfect mixture of instruction and amusement, the General Knowledge Paper.*

> *With all the skill but none of the labour of an itinerant*
> *vendor of quack medicines, he imposes on his readers a taste*
> *for general information. The reader enjoys this. He is stimu-*
> *lated by emulation, and, discovering that* Paracelsus *is a*
> *poem and not a Derby winner, fancies himself to be halfway*
> *to a professorship.*

Robertson-Glasgow went on to note that newspaper editors were restrained by the policies of their proprietors and, in wartime, additionally by national security. Neither of those is so firm a brake these days. Patriotic obligation has withered and today's press barons are kittens compared to Beaverbrook and Northcliffe. Anti-press lobbyists such as Hacked Off, who argue that newspapers are not accountable, like to ask '*quis custodiet ipsos custodes?*' Today, with newspapers in peril and power having shifted to social media, it would be more accurate to say '*custodiae derelictae sunt*'. One of the reasons public nincompoops get away with so much bossy hypocrisy may be that the press is no longer strong. Harry and Meghan complain about the malignant sway of the fourth estate but it has not stopped them misbehaving. The power of newspapers was probably always overstated, anyway. Readers buy papers not for the leader columns (hardly!) but for the puzzles, obituaries, horoscopes and, naturally, the theatre reviews and parliamentary sketches. To return to R. C. Robertson-Glasgow:

> *The man who reads the* News Chronicle, *say, is not going to*
> *chuck it over for the* Daily Mail, *say, because the* Daily Mail
> *reports the Rationing of Pepper and the Return to*

Constitutional Monarchy in Spain, while the News Chronicle *reports neither. The reader is far more likely to say, 'To hell with pepper – and Spain,' and pass on to the Racing, Soccer, or Cricket; or, in the case of a lady, to the latest photograph of a Princess dancing with a Guards Officer.*

If he wrote that today, he'd be sacked before lunchtime for upsetting the Me Too lobby.

(B)risk Business

Landslips can occur at night, when no one is looking. You go to bed thinking everything is fine; you wake up to a mess and wonder how it can ever be repaired. The same is true of two facets of bossiness: health and safety rules, and risk assessment.

The Health and Safety Executive (HSE) was conceived in the Health and Safety at Work Act 1974. Its daddy was the then employment secretary, Michael Foot, and its concerns were chiefly heavy industrial, relating to hazardous materials, factory fires and workplace accidents. It was the era of pit strikes – and pit deaths. Not just pits. Twenty-eight people were killed at the Flixborough chemical plant explosion in June 1974. Over the years the HSE has done plenty of good things to reduce such deaths. And yet 'health and safety' has become a wearisome national joke. Why? Because fools have used it overstringently, exaggerating concerns. It has become the tool – a word these people love – of spoilsports. Take the ban on graduation-day students throwing caps in the air because 'someone might get hurt' by a falling mortar board. The mayor of Maidstone was instructed to remove a little flag from her official car because it might cause someone an injury. A BBC studio told women in the audience at a music show not to throw undies on stage during a Tom Jones tribute act because the bloke playing Tom might trip on them and do himself a nasty injury. Cheshire police told all its officers to go on a cycling proficiency test before they could use a bicycle on work duties. You know the sort of thing.

The word 'safety' was worn thin during the Covid crisis. Matt Hancock used it repeatedly to justify constraints on our freedoms. 'Safety' was uttered with a look of drippy concern. Be not fooled. It was being appropriated to enforce stinkingly authoritarian measures. Strangers, in emails, would close with 'stay safe'. I soon took the decision to deny my custom to any firm urging me to 'stay safe' or 'keep well'. Apart from the political echoes – the subtle pressure such remarks created, showing that the sender believed the government's campaign of fear – there was the overfamiliarity. My health was none of their damn business.

Trade unions are good and bad on health and safety. They can represent collective bargaining at its noblest, labour uniting to force neglectful bosses to fix potentially fatal dangers in factories. But they have also often played health and safety as a political chip to create jobs for their shop stewards. What the unions probably didn't expect was the way the private sector has leapt on health and safety. Endless courses and consultants have sprung up, many of them making a mint out of the public sector. For a *Panorama* programme on health and safety a few years ago, I attended a ladder awareness course which told us how to use ladders. The bloke in charge was terribly excited about being filmed and vaingloriously mounted a stepladder – promptly bonking his head on the ceiling. The Beeb wouldn't let us use the footage because 'it might not be fair' on the old fool.

My wife, a piano teacher, gives lessons to Herefordshire prep-school children. Before being allowed to teach them she had to do a safeguarding course that told her about female genital mutilation and African breast-flattening. It told her she 'might need to talk about this' with pupils. The course also gave her a warning that she might find the material distressing. She actually just thought it bloody annoying and a waste of time.

The Health and Safety Executive is at its best when it sticks to the business of enforcing the law. It is less convincing when it tries to stir up engagement between managers and the workforce, sniffing out greater influence and work for itself and its hundreds of well-paid personnel. It has an online 'safety climate tool' which has been 'carefully designed by scientists'. This will help a firm's 'safety culture', we are told. That use of 'scientists' set off my inner bullshit-detector. What? A bunch of boffins in white coats crowded round this 'safety climate tool', examining its cogs and wheels? The 'safety climate tool' is available in forty-eight languages including Icelandic. At last count there were just over 2,000 Icelanders in Britain. How many of them did not speak English? The HSE also has a 'stress indicator tool', a 'line manager competency indicator tool' and an 'indicator tool manual', i.e., a tool for those baffled by tools. Ashes to ashes. Tools to tools. A whole new language has been invented. The health and safety sector tells directors that they need to 'set goals and get buy-in with senior managers' to secure 'data sources' for 'employee engagement' and 'sickness absence metrics' and 'intervention strategies to achieve excellence'. Monitoring health and safety has become a jargon-laden business and adds enormously to, oh no, the stress of life. I'm stressed, Doris, where's me tool?

Risk assessment dates back to 1992 and the Management of Health and Safety at Work Regulations, a statutory instrument (i.e., imposed by ministers without a Commons vote). The employment minister this time was a strong Thatcherite, Michael Forsyth. He recalls that risk assessments were seen as a way round all the impedimenta of health and safety rules. The idea was that a business owner could just say, 'Yes, I did assess those risks,' and would be legally secure. Officialdom soon put paid to that. *Protocols* for risk assessments were demanded. *Written proof* of risk assessments would be required. *Best practice* would be established. A whole new tier of bureaucracy was thus, accidentally, created. There are risk-assessment audits and guidelines, frameworks and reviews, dose-response risk analysis, dynamic risk, risk-exposure quantification and an entire thread of mathematics devoted to measuring risk versus loss. More people now work in risk assessment than work in coal mines. Risk assessments are now demanded for the most mundane and routine matters such as changing the light bulbs in a corridor. You're going to use a ladder? You'll need a certificate to say you've been on a ladder course. *Ouch!* Oh dear, did you, too, hit your head on the ceiling?

(B)risk Business

Westminster and Brussels (RIP) have made a thicket of legislation out of health and safety. The New Testament has four gospels, the Torah five books, Hinduism four Vedas. Here are just some of the statutes on health and safety:

Health and Safety at Work Act 1974.

Health and Safety Information for Employees Regulation 1989.

Safety Representatives and Safety Committees Regulation 1977.

Health and Safety (Consultation with Employees) Regulations 1996.

Management of Health and Safety at Work Regulations 1999.

Workplace (Health, Safety and Welfare) Regulations 1992.

Working Time Regulations 1998.

Health and Safety (Display Screen Equipment) Regulations 1992.

Personal Protective Equipment at Work Regulations 1992.

Provision and Use of Work Equipment Regulations 1998.

Manual Handling Operations Regulations 1992.

Health and Safety (First Aid) Regulations 1981.

The Health and Safety Information for Employees Regulations 1989.

Employers' Liability (Compulsory Insurance) Act 1969.

Reporting of Injuries, Diseases and Dangerous Occurrences Regulations 1995.

Noise at Work Regulations 1989.

Electricity at Work Regulations 1989.

Control of Substances Hazardous to Health Regulations 2002.

Chemicals (Hazard Information and Packaging for Supply) Regulations 2002.
Construction (Design and Management) Regulations 1994.
Gas Safety (Installation and Use) Regulations 1994.
Control of Major Accident Hazards Regulations 1999.
Dangerous Substances and Explosive Atmospheres Regulations 2002.
Control of Asbestos Regulations 2012.
Control of Lead at Work Regulations 2002.
Control of Substances Hazardous to Health Regulations 2002.
Chemicals (Hazard Information for Packaging and Supply) Regulations 2002.
Confined Spaces Regulations 1997.
Construction (Design & Managements) Regulations (CDM) 2007.
Control of Vibration at Work Regulations 2005.
Dangerous Substances and Explosive Atmospheres Regulations 2002.
Gas Safety (Management) Regulations 1996.
Highly Flammable Liquids and Liquefied Petroleum Gases Regulations 1972.
Ionising Radiations Regulations 1999.
Lifting Operations and Lifting Equipment Regulations 1998.
Lifts Regulations 1997.
Pressure Systems Safety Regulations 2000.
Simple Pressure Vessels (Safety) Regulations 1991.
Supply of Machinery (Safety) Regulations) 2008.
Work at Height Regulations 2005.

(B)risk Business

The 1992 regulations that brought in risk assessments made stipulations about the size and cleanliness of work stations, the conditions of floors, the cleanliness of windows and the provision of lavatories and clothes lockers in workplaces. If I were an astronaut, I'd sue.

Jobbery

Stuart Hibberd preparing to take his unconscious-bias test

Stuart Hibberd (1893–1983) was the BBC announcer who in 1935 told wireless listeners that 'the life of the King is moving peacefully to its close'. Ten years later he had a less melancholy duty when delivering the newsflash: 'German radio has just announced that Hitler is dead, I'll repeat that . . .' Hibberd was the BBC's chief announcer. He had a perfect radio voice for the era. It was clear, calm, and resonated with reassurance. You might suppose he was picked from a large number of applicants for the job but that was not the case. In his memoir, *This Is London ...* , Hibberd, who had been an Army officer in the First World War, describes how he was recruited to the BBC in 1924:

> *I had answered an advertisement in the* Morning Post *for a vacancy on the staff of the BBC and this led to an interview. I remember how my heart thumped as I walked up the steps of 2 Savoy Hill and saw on my left the large polished brass plate informing me that this was the Registered Office of the British Broadcasting Company, Ltd. I was received most politely by Arbuckle, the commissionaire, who asked me what my business was ... Soon afterwards I was being conducted into 'the presence'. Admiral Carpendale, a slim, lithe, blue-eyed, good-looking man, about 5 feet and 9 inches in height, shook hands with me and waved me to a chair, having a good look at me as he did so. He proceeded to ask me about my education and war service, my hobbies, my likes and dislikes, any special qualification I had, what games I played, and so on, and soon came to the conclusion that I was not the man they were then looking for because I had had no journalistic experience. At his suggestion, however, I agreed that my name should remain on the company's books, and this led to a second interview which resulted in my appointment as an assistant announcer in London. I remember that at this second interview, the 'Admiral' gave me a reading test, and afterwards asked me various questions. To these I replied quietly, being rather nervous, and he turned on me and said 'Speak up, man, and don't mumble.'*

Vice-Admiral Charles Carpendale was controller of the BBC. Given that he started his naval career in a ship with rigging and three decks of cannon, it is slightly pointless calling him old-school. Did he give Hibberd the job because he approved of his hobbies or the games he played, or because he had a shrewd idea for talent? Maybe the old tusker was simply relieved that Hibberd had not responded as another interviewee of that time did. Harry Pepper, a light music composer, went to Carpendale about a job and Carpendale barked at him, 'How old are you?' Pepper, in reply: 'Forty-four. How old are you?'

Bagging a BBC job these days is a lengthier procedure. I write as one who in the 1980s and 1990s went for about twenty BBC job interviews and failed the lot. They nowadays involve a board, so that no single person takes a decision. Human resources investigate the minority credentials of each applicant. No 'barking' at candidates is permitted. They are offered a hot drink, cosseted, counselled, asked if they have any worries and are generally mumsied. We are swallowing you into our maw. You are owned even before you have a job here. This is not just a BBC thing. Many big organisations behave this way.

It starts with the job adverts, which are manipulated to ooze false sincerity – at the expense of clarity. The new game at present is removing 'unconscious bias'. A consultancy called Totaljobs looked at 77,000 job adverts and found that many carried 'gender bias', and therefore served 'to unintentionally uphold gender stereotypes' (not to mention split infinitives). The following words were allegedly male-gendered: active, adventurous, challenge, compete, confident, decision, determined, independent, individual, lead, persist, principle, self-confident.

Other words were supposedly female-gendered. Here they are: commit, connect, considerate, dependable, honest, interpersonal, interdependent, kind, modesty, nurture, pleasant, polite, responsible, together.

What the hell has feminism been about all these years if our daughters don't feel they can lead and be persistent? Anyone really upset about such things must be so wet as to be barely worth employing.

What's going on here? Truthful analysis or some low-grade bullshit to try to make employment consultants seem indispensable? The BBC has fallen for it, naturally. Its news website ran an article which began: 'Words matter. And the way we use them in job adverts can dictate whether or not people bother to apply. This is a big problem.' Oh please. Famines, AIDS, *The Times* jumbo crossword: those are big problems. Not this. Two of the sources for this credulous report were the chief executive of a Seattle-based 'augmented writing software' company and the 'global head of diversity and belonging' of an Australian software firm, both of whom were shown in photographs. Who said there was no advertising on the BBC?

Unconscious-bias training has become the must-have thing – and if you are a major firm and you *don't* agree to spend thousands of pounds on it, you can expect to be castigated and accused of -isms. But has the high-water mark been passed? In late 2020, the Johnson government announced that it was not going to spend any more public money on unconscious-bias training, having discovered – you don't say, Jose – that it brought absolutely no benefit. The House of Commons hands over wads of public cash to a company that used a giant blue puppet to symbolise unconscious bias. Words such as 'lady', 'pensioner' and 'asylum seeker' are denounced as offensive. The firm involved, Challenge Consultancy, has been paid some £700,000 for these and other insights. When Tory MP Ben Bradley refused to attend such a course he was denounced by Lord Woolley who said this sort of training would make him a 'better politician'. Mr Bradley is elected. Lord Woolley made it into the unelected House of Lords by making a nuisance of himself in minority-identity politics.

Job allocation has been taken out of the hands of admirals and entrusted to self-promoting burblers who create problems that don't exist, berating us for faults that are only opportunities – for them. During the black-power protests of mid-2020, employment consultants jumped on them. Parade your conscience. Tweet your concern. In the head-hunting world we had the spectacle of a man called Mike Drew, 'partner and global head of Odgers Berndtson Executive Search's Global Technology Practice' filming an 'at home interview' with some American client in which the two of them talked about the 'absolutely critical journey' of diversity and inclusion, Mike looking all concerned and preaching about how the year had brought a 'much-needed spotlight on social injustices'. Inclusive environments, employee resource groups, affinity networks, lived experiences, the right intentional actions, reverse mentoring opportunities – it was all there. Anyone normal watching might well have concluded that Mike was not so much an in-touch kinda guy as a prize time-waster chasing political fashion out of corporate self-interest.

And we now go over to Stuart Hibberd at Broadcasting House. 'German radio has just announced that common sense is dead. I'll repeat that . . .'

Dusty Springfield would not have stood for it. Her songs included a cover of Lesley Gore's 'You Don't Own Me' (lyrics by John Madara and David White), which should perhaps be the official backing track to this book.

'And don't tell me what to do
Don't tell me what to say . . .'

Bunch of Naves

The new Delia

You can argue that the Church's very function is to instruct us. The Ten Commandments are unequivocal: thou shalt not do this and that. In Exodus chapter 20, those laws are reported in 350 words, about half the length of a newspaper parliamentary sketch. The author (God) does not labour the point. Brevity is a gift, succinctness a blessing. The simpler the instructions, the more likely they will be followed.

The Parish Safeguarding Handbook, issued in 2017 by the Church of England's house of bishops, is a longer read. It runs to seventy-four illustrated pages. For a publication whose purpose is telling volunteers how to spot child abusers, the cover is bland. It features anonymised, digitised blobs representing humans. 'Promoting a Safer Church' runs the subtitle. A less milky way of putting that would be: 'Stopping Pederasts'. Starker language might reinforce how unusual abusers are. The feebleness of busybodies' language normalises wickedness.

The handbook carries the cover blurb: 'With an introductory message from the Archbishop of Canterbury'. There you were in the bookshop, about to buy the latest Robert Harris thriller when your eyes alighted on that promise of an intro by Justin Welby. Sold! But when you open your parish handbook and turn to Archbishop Justin's prose in the expectation of glinting gems, you may experience a twinge of disappointment. Has authority ever been so prosaic? He tells us that to make churches safe we must all do 'a lot of hard work'. What he partly means is that we must undergo tedious training courses and comply with forms and procedures approved by him to assuage the insatiable monster of ecclesiastical bureaucracy. 'The Church will take appropriate steps', writes Welby. Is there a weaselier word than 'appropriate'? He wants us to offer support to abusers. At this point you wish you had bought the Robert Harris thriller. In thrillers, baddies come to sticky ends. In the modern Church, baddies are offered support by dreebling do-gooders. If the abusers only realised they might have to spend hours with hand-wringing, Lib-Dem-voting happy-clappies smiling

moonily at a bearded freak plinking a guitar while singing 'Forgiveness is the good Lord's gravy', they might
have stuck to stamp-collecting.

Until recently I belonged to our village's PCC, or paro-
chial church council. This sounds grander than it is. For
an idea of what a PCC does, think of those meetings in
the *Vicar of Dibley* when Jim said 'yes, yes, yes, no' and
Frank took the minutes and Owen talked about his flatu-
lence. Our PCC was composed of decent people who
were not too much like the Dibley gang but their/our
duties were the same: arranging services and events at the
church, keeping its roof waterproof and its graveyard
mown and generally maintaining an idea of church
community through the annual fête, carol service, harvest
festival and occasional knees-up. Belonging to the PCC
was a minor chore but someone has to do these things
and the clergy could not run the Church without PCC
members. Not that the bishops have yet conceded that
view.

Why did I quit? Two moments. We were told we could
not continue as members unless we attended a morning-
long course on 'safeguarding', i.e., child protection. We
would need to attend a workshop run by the diocese
safeguarding supremo. It was up to us: attend such a
lecture or surrender our (elected) membership of the
PCC. Obey or you're out. God bless you, too. Breaking
the habit of years, I did as pressed. About fifteen of us
duly gathered in a local church for one of these courses.
The average age must have been above seventy. Our
friend Liz was in the front row. She was 100. Others
included an Austrian countess, a retired senior surveyor

and his wife, a retired businessman and his wife and a devoted equestrian. We all knew each other but none of us had previously encountered the retired policewoman who was giving the C1 Learning and Development Framework Safeguarding Core Module. And yet she managed to make us feel small. She lectured us for four hours about sex crimes. 'I believe no one, I tend to suspect the worst in people,' she jabbered in that staccato, world-weary manner used by the Law when giving a memorised spiel. The message was couched in jargon and euphem-isms but it was an alarming one: everyone who arrived at our church was a potential child abuser and it was our duty – our corporate duty as tribunes of a Church that might otherwise be sued – to regard all worshippers as potential criminals. They might be octogenarians. They might be your own parents and they might give thou-sands of pounds to charity but *why* were they doing that? We should be sceptical at all times. We should monitor their every move and our snouts should twitch with suspicion. We should place a big notice about child abus-ers on our church noticeboard. We should keep a logbook of our suspicions and 'share our concerns', which is modern-speak for 'sneak on your neighbours'. We should never leave any vulnerable person alone with another human being, and that included letting the terminally ill receive communion in bed from unaccompanied priests. Nor should priests be allowed, on their own, to hear confessions – one of the most serious duties of a priest – because *something dreadful* might happen. Expect the worst. Always.

> When my friend Peter became a curate in Yorkshire in 1970, the Diocese of Ripon was administered by former Squadron Leader Driver and his assistant Elsie. When Peter retired in London in 2015 he consulted the Diocesan Handbook and found ninety-three functionaries listed. 'Most of them,' he said, 'were paid more than the parish clergy.'

By now I was certainly feeling abused and I was not alone, although centenarian Liz in the front row had drifted off to sleep. The retired police officer had told us to 'suspect the worst in people' and sure enough I was suspecting the worst of people like her. Unfairly, perhaps, I suspected them of jumping on a small number of sex-abuse cases to whip up anxiety, all to create work for themselves. The Church now spends a fortune on safeguarding and it was giving this retired policewoman the power to lecture middle-class bumblers who looked like extras from *Midsomer Murders*. We were handed leaflets about 'safeguarding strategy' and 'action plans', a diocesan working group, independent safeguarding audits and 'expert safeguarding professionals' at Church House. Further reading was suggested: that much-thumbed bestseller, 'Responding to Domestic Abuse,' and 'Responding Well to Those Who Have Been Sexually Abused'. You can forget about enjoying that Barbara Pym novel. Instead you must learn to 'manage safeguarding concerns' (the verb 'manage' has become aggressively active and means 'follow procedures laid down by *us*, the boss class'). We should all 'formally adopt national safeguarding policy and practice guidelines on a yearly basis' – i.e., pay annual obeisance to these strident creeps, reinforcing them in their secular pulpits. We were told that insurance companies would refuse to pay claims unless we obeyed the national safeguarding policy and practice guidelines as mentioned in the Safeguarding and Clergy Discipline Measure 2016. Wake up, Liz there in the front. Pay attention to legislation! Stop dreaming of the years when you and your generation fought to make Britain free from tyranny. As ever, the lawyers and the small-print merchants and niggle ninnies were flexing their pincers, bulging their compact eyes, filling their greedy maws, feasting off misfortune. Do, do, do as we say, or you will regret it, petty simpletons.

I left that event filled with what I feared were unchristian feelings. My temper boiled. Damn them and their horrible insistence on thinking the worst. If we suspect everyone else of being a child-molester, how will we ever send our toddlers to nursery? How will we drop them off at a birthday party or let them sit on Father Christmas's knee at the department store? Pursue that thinking and you will soon wonder if there is any point being a member of the human race. And yet this was being done by my Church.

And then came Archbishop Welby's response to the coronavirus pandemic. He and the Archbishop of York closed shop. Slam went the doors. No praying allowed. Entry forbidden. They might as well have erected yellow danger posters with the skull and crossbones. Churches had stayed open throughout the plagues of the Middle Ages, when priests ministered to the afflicted and often caught the plague themselves. Churches had continued to offer comfort to souls throughout the Civil War

– sometimes in brave defiance of Cromwellian thugs, as happened at Hereford Cathedral in 1645 when Dean Croft confronted soldiers from his pulpit and they nearly shot him. London's churches continued to hold services during the Blitz, cassocked vergers quietly lighting candles while outside the fire brigade battled blazes. Yet now, in 2020, church doors were chained and not even priests were allowed inside to say the daily offices. Bishops explained that they were worried about congregations infecting one another. This might be understandable from the Society for People Suffering Obsessive-Compulsive Disorder. But a church is where you go to contemplate mortality and parley with destiny. Churches, with their tombs and cold flagstones and flickering votive candles, help many of us come to terms with death. Welby and Co. were behaving as if human nature was wrong and as if our efforts over the years to keep churches open had been pointless. We had the spectacle, on Easter Day, of the archbishop conducting a service from his kitchen. Visible in shot: his electric kettle, his plug sockets. The Church establishment cooed. It told us the archbishop was showing that God could be found everywhere. This may have worked for those with strong faiths, but a Church is little use if it only preaches to the ardent. For those of us with wobblier faiths, Welby in his kitchen just looked like a cut-price Delia Smith.

In closing churches, the bishops went further than what ministers had expected. The prelates were desperate to be thought part of civil government and thus exceed its fervour for lockdown. Please, Miss, can we, too, be ink monitors? Eventually the government relaxed some measures and we were told churches would be allowed to reopen on 15 June 2020. When I heard that, I felt emotional. I emailed one of our church wardens and said how much I was looking forward to being allowed to sit alone again in our beautiful old church and murmur lines from Thomas Cranmer's Book of Common Prayer, which we still use despite widespread disapproval of its peerless pages by go-ahead clergy. But it was not to be. With regret, the warden said the church bureaucracy had issued the following form:

SCHEDULE OF WORK AND CLEANING REQUIRED TO BE COMPLETED BEFORE YOUR CHURCH CAN RE-OPEN FOR PRIVATE INDIVIDUAL PRAYER

In accordance with best practice and Government and Church of England Guidelines would you please attend to the listed work, fully complete this schedule and sign and return it if you want your church to re-open. On receipt of your schedule the required sanitising products, track and trace forms and signage will be put into your church.

Do not worry if this timescale is not feasible – 15 June is not mandatory – just attend to the work when you can and on receipt of the schedule we will put the finishing touches to your church to allow you to safely re-open.

Please note that the preparation must only be done by 1 person

Bunch of Naves

Name of church	
Name of cleaner	
Name and contact details of person(s) unlocking/locking daily	
TASKS	*INITIAL and √*
Allocate and sanitise two chairs or pew to be used for private prayer – place in view of the altar	
Rope off or otherwise prevent access to all other forms of seating	
Appropriately prevent access to organ and or piano	
All books and bookcases covered or put out of reach/touch	
All toys etc. put out of reach/sight	
Appropriately discourage access to pulpit	
Appropriately discourage access to lectern	
Appropriately prevent access to bell tower (if applicable)	
Take down prayer station and leave component parts at the back of church for collection	
Remove all candles from sight – no candles may be lit when churches re-open	
Remove any pre-closure flowers	

211

Change altar frontal and pulpit falls to green or white/all season according to your tradition	
Close altar rail and sanitise	
Lock kitchen or prevent access (if applicable)	
Lock toilets (if applicable)	
ON LEAVING THE CHURCH SANITISE ALL DOOR HANDLES TOUCHED INSIDE AND OUT	

That was it. I quit.

Bossy people love jargon because it is hard to understand and thus allows them to stand a level above the people they are addressing. Jargon excludes non-insiders. It tightens the club. The Army loves jargon, particularly acronyms (from PLDC for Primary Leadership Development Course to KFS for Knife, Fork and Spoon). So do scientists and accountants and lawyers. Modern churchgoers have also fallen for jargon. The following advertisement appeared in October 2020 and was placed by the diocese of Oxford, whose bishop is Steven Croft. The Rt Rev. Croft used to be team leader of a tambourine-rattling outfit called Fresh Expressions. His advert for a 'new congregations enabler' certainly used some fresh expressions.

New Congregations Enabler
*Do you have experience of growing new worshipping communities through church planting or fresh expressions?

The Oxford Diocese wants to see a thriving mixed ecclesial economy. To help achieve this there is an innovative church planting and fresh expressions programme with a significant investment of £4.5 million, aiming to grow 750 new worshipping communities of all shapes and sizes over the next decade. This will be done be creating and facilitating Greenhouses (as part of the national Greenhouse initiative) containing up to ten mission initiatives in each.

We are seeking to appoint a New Congregations Enabler who will

*Encourage the growth of new congregations through the creation of a minimum of twenty Greenhouses over five years.

*Mentor and coach these new Greenhouses as they emerge, requiring sensitivity to local contexts and emergent initiatives, nurturing them into sustainable worshipping communities.

Hours: 37 hours a week

Salary: £34,914 to £37,600

There is a Genuine Occupational Requirement (GOR) under Part 1 Schedule 9 of the Equality Act 2010 for the post holder to be a practising Christian. We particularly welcome applications from Black, Asian and Minority (BAME) candidates.

Oxford is where Cranmer was martyred. It was once the centre of the High Church Oxford Movement. It has some of the brightest people in England. Yet now they are to be ministered to in greenhouses? Does that make congregations vegetables – or fruits, even?

'Enabler' has become a popular term for Church recruiters. The diocese of Coventry was next. It was looking for a:

Reconciliation Enabler

35 hours a week Monday to Friday with some evening and weekend working. £37,770 per annum plus 8.5% employer pension contributions.

The Diocese of Coventry is seeking to appoint a full-time Reconciliation Enabler to work towards the objective of equipping the whole Diocese for the work of reconciliation. This is a new expression of our partnership with the Archbishop of Canterbury's Reconciliation Ministry and is a jointly funded post. The main responsibilities are: Work closely with the Archbishop's reconciliation team to mobilise, envision, equip and empower churches and individuals to engage with the movement of reconciliation and run the Difference course. This will include networking with ecumenical partners ... steering the diocese through the Living in Love and Faith process and developing 'courageous Coventry conversations' in areas of societal need and tension.

You might think that enablers are vicars on the cheap. Hardly. These advertisements offered salaries well above the c.£25,950 benchmark stipend paid to parish priests in 2019. It was also higher than the money paid to archdeacons (£35,400). Priests tend to devote more than thirty-seven hours a week to their duties. They also work 'weekends', or on the Sabbath, as it was once called. These enablers were being placed above priests in the Church hierarchy and the management-speak of the advertisements showed where they would sit in the firmament: on the right-hand side of the professionalised lay executive.

And these power-mad manglers of the English language dare to accuse the Book of Common Prayer of being inaccessible.

What discord there was about a song. The BBC decided its Last Night at the Proms concert, traditionally a night of not entirely serious patriotism, should be altered. The singalong of 'Rule Britannia' should be dropped because it was tainted by a mention of slaves. Middle Britain erupted in protest at this bossy edict and the Beeb's director-general, Lord Hall, a master of reverse ferrets, changed the ruling. Not everyone was pleased with him. Cat Lewis, an executive producer of *Songs of Praise*, compared Rule Britannia enthusiasts to neo-Nazis singing 'we will never be forced into a gas chamber'.

I don't know it. Must be one of those modern hymns.

Arts Angst

Morgan Freeman: a great man

On American television fifteen years ago, the actor Morgan Freeman was interviewed by Mike Wallace of *Sixty Minutes*. Here is an extract from their conversation:

WALLACE: *Black History Month, you find . . .*

FREEMAN: *Ridiculous.*

WALLACE: *Why?*

FREEMAN: *You're going to relegate my history to a month?*

WALLACE: Come on.

FREEMAN:What do you do with yours? Which month is White History Month? Come on, tell me.

WALLACE: I'm Jewish.

FREEMAN: OK.Which month is Jewish History Month?

WALLACE:There isn't one.

FREEMAN:Why not? Do you want one?

WALLACE: No, no.

FREEMAN: I don't either. I don't want a Black History Month. Black history is American history.

WALLACE: How are we going to get rid of racism until . . . ?

FREEMAN: Stop talking about it. I'm going to stop calling you a white man. And I'm going to ask you to stop calling me a black man. I know you as Mike Wallace. You know me as Morgan Freeman.You're not going to say, "I know this white guy named Mike Wallace." Hear what I'm saying?

Racists judge people by the colour of their skin. They are obsessed with it. That happened in South Africa under apartheid and it happened in the United States, where until the 1960s there were separate restaurants, public lavatories and even graveyards for whites and black. Graveyards!

Now liberals do it, too. In 2018 I was accused of being racist by one of our national institutions, the Royal Shakespeare Company. The experience wasn't much fun. In a drama review I had questioned the colour-blind casting of a Restoration comedy staged by the RSC. *The Fantastic Follies of Mrs Rich* was written in 1700 by Mary Pix. The RSC did a period production with elaborate costumes and wigs. One of the characters, Clerimont, is a huntin', shootin' chump, that particularly English type of

Hooray that has probably knocked round these islands since the days of Alfred the Great. Clerimont should be a cracking comedy part but I didn't think the actor was suited to it. He was too cool, too handsome, too modern. In my review I asked if he had been chosen because he was black. The RSC had for some time been making a to-do about colour-blind casting, and one of its major providers of income, the Arts Council, had been campaigning for theatres to run 'blind' auditions – the idea being to increase parts for black actors. Occasionally the casting was clunky and this, I felt, was such an occasion. Whoomph. Up went an almighty hue and cry, with the RSC issuing a public statement attacking me as some sort of National Front lunatic and a slew of stage luvvies flaying me on social media and at the Olivier Awards a couple of nights later. The debate continued in my then paper, the *Daily Mail*, which devoted a two-page spread in which I put my side of the argument and the RSC's artistic director, Gregory Doran, put his.

I reprised my belief – hardly controversial, I had thought – that casting black actors in traditionally white roles, or women in traditionally male roles, sometimes worked and sometimes didn't. I had in the past praised instances when it was successful. It generally depended on whether or not the performance was believable. Dramatic truth is not the same as social engineering. Off the top of my head I can think of two black actors – Simon Trinder and Lenny Henry, someone whose stage career I have championed – who could have played Clerimont well in that production. But the guy they chose was wrong. Doran, on his side of the two-page spread, wrote that 'major actors playing major roles are cast not because of their heritage but for the simple reason that they are supremely talented performers. We don't cast actors because we want to tick any boxes but because they are right for the part.' I'd like to hear him state that on oath. Please note that he said 'major' actors were not cast for 'major roles' because of their heritage. That may have been a tacit admission that, fifteen years after Morgan Freeman's eloquent interview on *Sixty Minutes*, non-major actors are indeed judged by their heritage (i.e., colour). Which brings me back to what I said earlier. Racists are people who judge others by colour.

As for audiences, they are probably little fazed by the casting of black or white actors, provided it doesn't become a block to credibility. I have been to a *Twelfth Night* where one of the identical twins was white and one was non-white. Sorry, but with a plot that depends on other characters getting the twins mixed up, that was silly. When blind casting becomes noticeable – when the audiences feel they are being lectured – I dare say theatre-goers start to resent it and suspect the directors are subtly accusing *them* of harbouring some sort of race bias.

Some arts organisations spend an amazing deal of time and money anguishing about equality statistics. If you want to see a classic of the genre, visit the British Council's creative equity toolkit, which gives directors a guide to how to avoid casting solely on merit. Who benefits from this sort of thing? Black actors and artists? Not much. But bureaucrats and consultants are kept very much in work. Let's look at a study commissioned by the Arts Council in 2013 in order to 'shape its investment process' (i.e., spend taxpayers' money). The report was entitled 'Equality and Diversity within the Arts and Cultural Sector in England'. It was written by Consilium Research & Consultancy Ltd, a Tyneside company that described itself as 'a professional and dynamic organisation' devoted to 'civic participation' with an 'ethos fundamentally based on delivering rigorous consultancy services that are able to inform practice, shape policy and facilitate change'. The authors did not stint themselves. The report ran to ninety-nine pages full of charts and statistics about the race, gender, disability, age, sexual orientation, religious affiliation, marital status, socio-economic standing and pregnancy status of arts audiences. At the end there are conclusions for the Arts Council to ponder. These are as follows:

Undertake in-depth qualitative research to explore arts and cultural participation and attendance barriers and motivations among people with different disabilities, within different ethnic groups and at different ages.

Undertake in-depth qualitative research to explore gender-based tastes and preferences for arts and culture among boys and girls aged under fifteen, and the influence of parental behaviours on child participation.

Complete literature reviews and qualitative research to identify workforce development and change management models that support leaders within the sector to transform organisational cultures and develop a more equal and diverse workforce.

Undertake in-depth qualitative research on equality and diversity issues facing the protected groups of sexual orientation, religion and/or belief, pregnancy and maternity, marriage or civil partnership status and gender re-assignment.

Undertake additional quantitative data analysis of key datasets such as the Taking Part Survey, particularly across protected characteristics (e.g., by sexual orientation, ethnic groups within the 2011 census categories) where there has thus far been limited analysis.

Complete a focused literature review specifically on equality and diversity issues in relation to the library sector.

Translation: give more work to consultants rather than spending Arts Council money on the arts.

Those bastards who attacked me as a racist should have saved their bullets for the likes of Consilium. The 'blind' casting thing is a bureaucratic con which lectures blameless audiences and takes money away from arts practitioners, sticking it instead in the hands of consultants. As for Consilium? It was bought in 2018 by a bigger firm. Big fees all round no doubt – more than your average RSC actor can probably expect to earn in a decade.

The function of a national library is to catalogue, store and lend the written word. This allows historians to study what was published in the past. Librarians are not expected to like every book they stock. Their taste or politics should not matter. But in 2020 the managers of the British Library took it upon themselves to announce that the library was going to become an 'actively anti-racist organisation'. It was almost as if anyone not 'actively' anti-racist was a racist. The curators intended that the library would be 'truly representative in terms of its staff, collections and the users it serves'. What did this mean? How or why should a library be 'representative' of its staff? A working party was created to 'explore the full range of issues relating to systemic and other forms of racism, with a view to making recommendations for public and accountable actions, targets and time-frames'. There was an 'urgent and overdue need to reckon fully and openly with the colonial origins and legacy of some of the Library's collections'. Literary students might identify that as the sort of language used by Marxist revolutionaries.

Gulp. You might not want to be overdue on a book with this lot.

Five years ago I made a Radio 4 programme called 'What's the Point of the Met Office?' It was a jocular, half-hour documentary. At the Beeb's insistence I looked briefly (perhaps four minutes of the programme) at climate change and interviewed three MPs, one Labour, one Tory and one Scots Nat. Two said mildly sceptical things about man-made climate change. When it aired: *Sturm und Drang*! The BBC's environment analyst joined a yowling mob that claimed I was some type of climate-change denier. Utter balls, but a journalistic standards committee sat and (in my absence) found me guilty. My little show was wiped from the record. The bossocracy had expunged it, and me, from the record. The chairman of that committee was a man called Richard Ayre. Recently we learned that the BBC used seriously smelly-sounding tricks to persuade the late Princess of Wales to give Martin Bashir the interview that led to her tragic spiral out of the Royal Family. One of the journalists defending the methods used? Richard Ayre. Well, well, well.

Batty

Complaining about local housing eyesores is generally pointless. Planning officials will sneer at you for being a Nimby. Unless, unless . . . you can collect a pocketful of bat droppings. Sprinkle them round the site and now you're in business. Tip off the environmental gauleiters that the proposed building works will interfere with nesting pipistrelles. Wham. It'll stop the bulldozers like nothing else.

Bats are protected under the Habitats Regulations and the Wildlife and Countryside Act 1981. It may seem an obscure law but it has been used with extraordinary venom by single-issue busybodies. Removing bats is now harder than shifting gypsies. At the merest whiff of bat, and whiff is indeed the word, the Natural England quango will swoop on a building site. It farms out its inspection function to the Bat Conservation Trust, which has a dog (well, a bat) in the fight. Work may not continue without a survey and that survey involves payment to bat enthusiasts. Guess what: they often find evidence of bats. All sorts of expensive mitigations are demanded until building work can resume. Mitigations. It is the word of the year, a word shimmering with fusspot, middle-class interference.

Wildlife charities claim that bat numbers have dropped steeply in Britain. Do we believe them? Woodland has been returning to our island at a surprising rate in the past half-century. Much of Britain is now as tree-covered as it was in the year 1300, although you seldom hear that reported. Good news is not what campaigners want to spread. Good news might dent their income and job prospects. Most bats roost in trees and with all those new trees, bats must be spoilt for accommodation. They also like houses, barns and churches. Indeed, they have made many churches near-unusable, and there is little that can be done to eject them.

I quite like bats. They eat a lot of midges and they are good to watch at twilight, swooping and diving. There is something timeless about bats. My wife the church organist feels less benevolent towards them because they once nearly killed her. Bats flew around her in the organ loft where she practised. She became dangerously ill with viral meningitis. The doctors said they suspected she had been infected by bats. More than five years later, she still suffers side effects.

Bat pee stinks. At Sleaford, Lincs, church volunteers have a constant battle to keep the pews and altar clean from bat mess. Prayer books and hymnals are wrecked. The church has a medieval mural and a thirteenth-century effigy which have been wrecked by the bats. Hassocks are spoiled and in 2017 an eight-year-old girl had a bat fall on her head. They had a job removing it from her hair. Lord Cormack told the House of Lords of another incident at a church in Herefordshire's Golden Valley where the priest was about to administer the bread and wine when a bat flew overhead and dropped its bombs. Bat crap with your communion wafer, Mrs Beamish? There are stories of bat droppings corroding ancient brasses and making such a smell that congregations – even before the Covid horrors – had to wear masks. Cormack begged parliament to consider a short Bill allowing churches to exempt themselves from the 1981 law which made it illegal to disturb bats. The May government didn't want to know; a similar initiative currently before the Commons looks doomed. Politicians won't take on the bat lobby because they are frightened of being accused of animal cruelty. Lobby terrorism strikes again.

Animal-rights activists love animals. They are not always so keen on humans. The Unite trade union has alleged 'bullying of staff members from the very top' at the RSPCA. Not that RSPCA executives are mean to themselves. The top bods are paid six-figure salaries, and in 2018 it was reported that one of them had been given a £200,000 pay-off. Enough to live off steak tartare for years. The charity's chief executive's annual biscuits are £150,000 a year. Think of that, next time you are given a begging leaflet with pictures of sad-eyed puppies or hollow-ribbed donkeys. In 2014 the World Animal Protection charity paid one employee £231,732 in salary and redundo. Dogs Trust is one of those charities that has campaigned against hunting and it has duly won itself plenty of publicity, and income. In 2018 it ran a campaign showing a sorrowful mutt standing next to an empty food cupboard. Please help feed Fido. In that same period the Trust spent over £1 million on executives' pay. The *Daily Mirror* reported that in the preceding decade the income of Dogs Trust increased by 73 per cent but the number of dogs it cared for rose by less than 10 per cent.

Why don't protestors complain about this? Instead, they take to Twitter to decry as a sadist anyone who opposes them. Dairy farmers think badgers spread bovine tuberculosis? Dairy farmers are profiteering, murderous bastards! So say the bunny-huggers, who have probably never met a cow. These ostensibly kindly souls will send razor blades through the post to scientific researchers whose human life-saving work may involve killing rats. They will break into mink farms and release the inmates, which then go and slaughter wildlife. Employees at Huntingdon Life Sciences had their cars destroyed, their homes spray-painted – 'Drop HLS or you will be dead!' – and family graves desecrated by animal-rights extremists, who also tried to bring pressure on the company's suppliers. There is a feral desire to kill opposition to their cause and MPs swallow it because they lack the backbone to say no to emotional black-mailers. The animal-rights zealots are as single-minded as ferrets in attack mode. This is the attitude of radicals across the board: animal rights, climate activism, nationalism, anti-abortionism. One's sympathies were tested when Jolyon Maugham QC, himself one of life's priggish ultras (against Brexit), had a nasty Basil Brush with obsessive activism. Our Jolyon came unstuck after he tried to deal with a fox in his chicken house one Boxing Day. The great lawyer set about the intruder with a baseball bat and was incautious enough to mention this on Twitter. Oooh-là-là, what a ding-dong ensued. Animal-rights keenies fell on their mobiles to issue feverish denunciations on social media. To make things even worse, Maugham had been dressed in a kimono at the time of the atrocity. It was just as well Maugham hadn't found Nigel Farage canvassing at his front door or we might have had another Tony Martin case on our hands. But please put to one side the merriment of seeing Farmer Jolyon undone by his own favourite weapon (I refer to Twitter, not the baseball bat). Was the monomaniacal

Jolyon Maugham and Basil Brush QC:
whack-whack, boom-boom!

QC really so out of order? Why was his vermin control any of our business? Likewise, why should it concern others when prayerful churchgoers try to deter bats? Is it really such a terrible thing if dairy farmers cull badgers? Maugham was trying to save his hens. Churches try to save souls. Farmers are trying to save their herds. The number of animal lives lost to bovine TB far exceeds those involved in a nocturnal sniper's badger cull. The protestors who moo and cluck are bossing us about for their own purposes. The world has gone bats.

Social Credit Crunch

There are two reasons not to jaywalk in China. First, you might be run over, for the Chinese are not always merciful drivers, particularly if running late for their elevenses. If faced with a choice between mowing down a pedestrian and running an amber light to get to the *baozi* dumplings stall in time, they may opt for the latter. Second, your social credit score could be affected. Your what? Your social credit score.

In some parts of China, citizens are issued with social credit scores. If they do something 'naughty', such as:

jay-walking,
mowing down jay-walkers,
playing music too loudly late at night,
eating on a Tube train,
failing to observe the correct recycling procedures,
settling a bill late,
spreading religion,
refusing to do military service,
lighting a fag in a no-smoking zone,
playing an excessive number of video games,
making frivolous purchases,

failing to keep Fenton on his lead or allowing him to
   bark . . .
 . . . they will lose points. On the other hand, if they give
do something that is considered helpful to the community, they will win points. This might include:
   volunteering,
   doing an heroic deed,
   giving to the poor,
   being kind to the mother-in-law.
Their running score will be kept on a database. If they
lose too many points, they may find that they will:
   encounter difficulty booking airline tickets,
   be barred from first-class railway compartments,
   their children will not be admitted to the best schools,
   jobs in banking or with the civil service may prove
      elusive,
   so may visas for foreign travel.
   Energy firms will charge them higher prices,
   they may have to pay more to ride public bikes,
   and kiss goodbye to that university place.
   Five-star hotels will decline their business,
   and, ruff luck, Fenton will be confiscated.
The social credit system began in 2014 with the
philosophy 'allow the trustworthy to roam everywhere
under heaven while making it hard for the discredited
to take a single step'. And that is the word that keeps
being used by Chinese officialdom about low scorers.
They are 'discredited'. The scheme's proposers argue
that 'keeping trust is glorious and breaking trust is
disgraceful'. At present it has only been tried in some
cities. Local governments hold the data and the idea is

that they will forward it to the National Credit Information Sharing Platform (NCISP) which, one day, may be able at the touch of a few buttons to gauge the social credit-worthiness of any one of the country's 1.4 billion inhabitants.

So far things have been low-key. I am told officials are using it simply to try to mould public sociability and stop inconsiderate behaviour. Maybe it will remain benign. 'Civilised families' are hailed in public, their photographs placed on public noticeboards rather as local newspapers in Britain will run snaps of people who have helped with the local anti-litter campaign. Could it happen here? Given the way officials have been trying to mould behavioural change, yes. Borrowers are already given credit-worthiness scores by credit assessment companies. Likewise, Facebook collects data on our interests, analyses our browsing habits and tailors its content accordingly. Supermarket apps monitor what goods we buy and create 'favourites' lists for us. It is not a huge leap from that to having the government handing out Tufty Club badges. They could call it, ooh, I don't know, maybe something like 'the honours system'.

Every so often it is reported that Whitehall wants to introduce digital ID cards. Critics fear that these centralised identity codes could be used to collect information on people's behaviour. Supporters of the Chinese social credit system argue that it is merely an incentive to thoughtful behaviour, a benevolent educational programme for a large country that still has plenty of inhabitants who need to be shown how to behave. But what if it fell into the hands of someone less benevolent than the Chinese Communist Party – someone, say, such as Matt Hancock, Nicola Sturgeon, or Sir Piers Morgan OMG. How might the scoring system work? You might find that you won points for:

voting in local elections,

tweeting in favour of vaccines,

giving up drink,

displaying a 'thank you NHS' rainbow in your window,

re-posting safety information notices on your social media feeds,

going vegetarian,

inviting a Syrian refugee to live in your home,

buying an electric car.

And you would lose points for:

singing along to 'Swing Low, Sweet Chariot' at Twickenham,

paying tradesmen in cash,

wearing a fur coat,

buying a second-hand diesel car,

smoking in the street,

stockpiling loo paper,

failing to wear a mask in town centres,

eating hamburgers,

calling your son Enoch.

We will close with a reassuring note of incompetence. Australia's ABC News contacted the Beijing authorities for comment about social credit. Back came the request that any press questions had to be submitted not by email or social media, but fax. The Aussies somehow dug out a fax from the back of the office cupboard and sent their request. They never received a reply. As you read this, the fax is still probably whirring away, shiny paper creaking as it slowly emerges into daylight.

Dunbossin'

At Mayfair book launches, when we had such things, you would see them in the corners of the ballroom: one-time beauties, the Zuleika Dobsons of their day, cheek bones still high but all else fading, the make-up brittle, eyes filmy. Fingers, knobbled by age, fiddled with the clasp of a handbag no longer in fashion. It happens to us all if we live long enough. Almost everything rots. Today's Tweeting tyro will be tomorrow's slippered dementia patient. Visit the House of Lords and you see yesteryear's cockerels in states of moulting decay.

Handbags are not the only things to go out of fashion. So do political systems and their once bossy enforcers. Pan-Slavism, Makhnovism, Mobutism, Strasserism . . . all came and went. The bossocrats who have recently made British life so neuralgic may at present seem insuperable but they will eventually lose their feathers. Let's hope it happens before we have had the old national virtue of bloody-mindedness completely beaten out of us.

The depressing thing about the last two years has been the extent to which Covid constraints were swallowed with so little demur, particularly at Westminster and in the media. Fleet Street's dissenters were quietly muzzled by editors terrified of losing government advertising. Broadcast journalists demanded tighter controls – 'more! more!' shrieked the suave absolutists of Sky News, Beth Rigby's eyeballs bulging with fervour. The only parliamentary opposition came from a few hairy impis on the Tory benches, shaking their tribal spears as the armour-plated convoy of lockdowners cruised past, sealed tight in their own superiority.

This sounds an odd thing to say but I am glad my father did not live to see all this. Perhaps unusually for a schoolmaster, he hated being told what do. My brother died, too – my handsome, life-affirming, cup-winning brother, who wrote in this book about the grimness of hospital wards. He was just 62. The care he received from the National Health Service was distinctly sub-optimal. When Alexander was terminally ill they tried to stop him discharging himself from hospital, four nurses crowding round him like ravens, one shoving a foot against the wheel of his stroller to block his escape while another told him he was breaking their health and safety guidelines. Only after he threatened them with his lawyer did they allow him home to die. He held a goodbye party first, though. No one wore a mask.

Reverence for regulations has become a fetish, a disease, for many an end in itself. But why should we encourage our children only to obey? Should we not also teach them when rules deserve to be broken? An English master at Eton tried that and he was banned (in a welcome turn-up for the books, the Teaching Regulation Agency later cleared him of any wrongdoing). Codes are no more impressive than the elites who impose them. One look at

Lady Hale in her spider brooch told us all we needed to know about the Supreme Court. One glance at Prof Neil Ferguson should have given us the measure of SAGE's stuffing. Can anyone honestly look at today's grievance advocates and not see that Big Diversity is every ounce as cynical as Big Tobacco or Big Pharma?

It is possible I have been a little bossy in this book. In time, the heat will pass. It may for the governing classes, too. Once they have made their point, seized back control or whatever it is that has so consumed them, they will retire to Dunpreachin' and the flame will slowly slacken. Let cheeerful scepticism then revive.

The miracle of civilisation is that, while we humans decay, it somehow preserves the beauty of individual and collective confidence. Civilisation is not a given. Each generation must keep that plate spinning. There are liver spots on my hands as I type this but if, one day, I am lucky enough to have grand-children, I hope I am still sufficiently *compos* to urge them to question the rules and, if necessary, tell their enforcers to hop it. The most important words in British English, apart from 'please', 'thank you' and 'more marmalade pudding' should be 'stop bloody bossing me about'.

Picture Credits

P.vi Reg Speller/Stringer/Getty Images
P.5 Shutterstock
P.15 Fine Art/Getty Images
P.21 Shutterstock
P.23 ClassicStock/Getty Images
P.27 PA/Shutterstock
P.34 PA Images/Alamy Stock Photo
P.37 BEN STANSALL/Getty Images
P.45 Royal Mint
P.62 (top) PA Images/Alamy Stock Photo
P.62 (bottom) ATA KENARE/Getty Images
P.65 Michael Curie/Alamy Stock Photo
P.68 Photograph by Derek Storm/Everett Collection/Mary Evans
P.73 Xinhua/Alamy Stock Photo
P.78 PA Images/Alamy Stock Photo
P.86 Shutterstock
P.88 Universal Images Group/Getty Images
P.91 (left) WPA Pool/Pool/Getty Images
P.91 (right) Radio Times/Getty Images
P.99 © UK Parliament/Mark Duffy Photography
P.103 iStock
P.110 Fairfax Media Archives/Getty Images
P.116 PA Images
P.123 (left) iStock
P.123 (right) Dorset Media Service/Alamy Stock Photo
P.126 Shutterstock
P.131 Imagno/Getty Images
P.136 Sean Sexton/Getty Images
P.147 John Downing/Getty Images
P.161 Doug Pizac/AP/Shutterstock
P.171 John Stillwell/Stringer/Getty Images
P.179 Harris/AP/Shutterstock
P.197 © BBC
P.202 Pictorial Press Ltd/Alamy Stock Photo
P.203 PA Images
P.217 Jacques BANAROCH/SIPA/Shutterstock
P.229 (top) Jeff J Mitchell/Getty Images
P.229 (bottom) Ken McKay/ITV/Shutterstock

Index

Index